D0934994

NUMBER THIRTEEN

Carolyn and Ernest Fay Series in Analytical Psychology

David H. Rosen, General Editor

The Carolyn and Ernest Fay edited book series, based initially on the annual Fay Lecture Series in Analytical Psychology, was established to further the ideas of C. G. Jung among students, faculty, therapists, and other citizens and to enhance scholarly activities related to analytical psychology. The Book Series and Lecture Series address topics of importance to the individual and to society. Both series were generously endowed by Carolyn Grant Fay, the founding president of the C. G. Jung Educational Center in Houston, Texas. The series are in part a memorial to her late husband, Ernest Bel Fay. Carolyn Fay has planted a Jungian tree carrying both her name and that of her late husband, which will bear fruitful ideas and stimulate creative works from this time forward. Texas A&M University and all those who come in contact with the growing Fay Jungian tree are extremely grateful to Carolyn Grant Fay for what she has done. The holder of the McMillan Professorship in Analytical Psychology at Texas A&M functions as the general editor of the Fay Book Series.

Ethics and Analysis

Ethics & Analysis

Philosophical Perspectives
and Their Application in Therapy

LUIGI ZOJA

Foreword by David H. Rosen

Texas A&M University Press   *College Station*

The paper used in this book
meets the minimum requirements
of the American National Standard for Permanence
of Paper for Printed Library Materials, Z39.48-1984.
Binding materials have been chosen for durability.

LIBRARY OF CONGRESS CATALOGING-IN-PUBLICATION DATA

Zoja, Luigi.
Ethics and analysis : philosophical perspectives and their application in therapy /
Luigi Zoja ; foreword by David H. Rosen. —1st ed.
p. cm. — (Carolyn and Ernest Fay series in analytical psychology ; no 13)
Includes bibliographical references and index.
ISBN-13: 978-1-58544-578-3 (cloth : alk. paper)
ISBN-10: 1-58544-578-9 (cloth : alk. paper)
1. Ethics. 2. Psychoanalysis. 3. Psychotherapy. I. Title.
BJ45.Z65 2007
174'.9150195—dc22
2006030027

To my Aunt Nella Zoja,

who tried to teach me as a child

what my school did not,

namely, the distinction

between justice & injustice

We're not of this world, you and I,
we're among the just.
Warmth was not meant for the likes of us.
May mercy come to the just!

—Dora to Kaliayev
in Act Three of *Les justes*, Albert Camus

Contents

Series Editor's Foreword

DAVID H. ROSEN

Through the new ethic, the ego-consciousness
is ousted from its central position in a psyche
organized on the lines of a monarchy or totalitar-
ian state, its place being taken by *wholeness* or the
Self, which is now recognized as central.

—C. G. Jung

Luigi Zoja has written a thought-provoking treatise on ethics and
analysis that advocates a healing "gray zone," or middle path. In Part
One, Zoja discusses ethics in general, focusing on its historical and
philosophical roots. He reveals how justice (ethics) and beauty (aesthetics) are linked and, ideally, in balance. He then emphasizes how
beauty and ethics have fallen apart, losing the original unity (*kalokagathia*) they possessed in classical antiquity. Thus, the disappearance
of beauty as an ideal has been accompanied—not incidentally—by
ugliness and immorality. Zoja suggests that ego consciousness and
the rule of law and rationality have attempted to fill the vacuum created by ethics and aesthetics being asunder. However, he posits that
this has only worsened the situation. Zoja calls out for us to confront
the shadow and develop an inner ethical and aesthetic sense and cultivate the ability to hold the tension of the opposites of good and evil.
He underscores the archetypal value of a "gray zone,"[1] which would
allow for a transcendent function to emerge leading to truth and reconciliation as well as transformation (similar to the consciousness

raising and forgiveness model of the post-Apartheid era in South Africa). He outlines how an individual, a society, and hopefully the world can go from immorality to morality and experience healing. Zoja promotes a "new ethic" based on depth psychology as described by Erich Neumann.[2] This is based on acknowledging the personal and collective shadow, and Zoja even coins a new word, "Endarkment," to counter our obsession with Enlightenment. As Neumann stated, "It is the paradoxical secret of transformation itself, since it is in fact in and through the shadow that the lead is transformed into gold. It is only when man learns to experience himself as the creature of a Creator who made light and darkness, good and evil, that he becomes aware of his own Self as a paradoxical totality in which the opposites are linked together as they are in the Godhead."[3]

In the West, Justice is symbolized by a female figure, originally Themis, the Greek Goddess of Justice and Law, which was changed in Roman mythology to Justicia, one of the four virtues along with Prudence, Fortitude, and Temperance.[4] Perhaps the patriarchal focus of Roman law and power contributed to how we view justice. For instance, one of the depictions of Justice at the United States Supreme Court reveals her clear-sighted with a huge sword at her side. However, the feminine essence of justice and ethics connects it to the anima and qualities of the soul. This is why Carol Gilligan emphasizes how moral development is different in girls and women.[5] She focuses on feminine caring as a quality of justice, differentiating this from masculine legality, or rule of law. Of course, it is really a both/and situation, where the heart (feeling) must always be in balance with the head (thinking). Also at the U.S. Supreme Court, both inside and outside the building, Justice is depicted in three sculptural groups with and without a blindfold. The origin of the blindfold is unclear, but it stems from the sixteenth century when artists increasingly showed Justice with a blindfold.[6] Was the blindfold added to indicate the court's impartiality or the court's tolerance of abuse of the law? Or was it added to mitigate the beauty of the naked body, which was so commonplace in ancient Rome and Greece? Regardless, given Luigi Zoja's consciousness raising view of justice and beauty, in the next part of this book Zoja takes off the blinders.

In Part Two of *Ethics and Analysis*, Zoja applies philosophical perspectives to therapy. He emphasizes Immanuel Kant's philosophy by focusing on its practical ethical imperative. In this situation, a person (or a patient in therapy or analysis) must never be used as an instrument or means of another individual's desires, as this is abusive and unethical. Zoja also underscores Max Weber's ethics of responsibility, which Zoja links to intentional and unintentional consequences. In other words, we are urged to confront the shadow deep in our unconscious thereby raising ethical consciousness.

In his important book, *Sex in the Forbidden Zone*, Peter Rutter describes how he almost used a patient as an instrument.[7] Fortunately he stopped himself from acting out and sublimated his neurosis into a research project that culminated in an outstanding book, one that can raise the consciousness of other therapists. Luigi Zoja claims, and I concur, that the core aim of analysis is ethical, as it does battle with lies. As we know, the truth is reality, and it sets you free. This is the whole basis of truth and reconciliation! Martin Buber underscores that the lie is a specific evil introduced by man. Buber states, "In a lie, the spirit practices treason against itself."[8] The lie makes modern man "crazy," as Buber rightly asserts; the person who lies speaks "delusion" from the position of an egotistical and selfish individual.[9] The person who tells the truth is humble, pure at heart, and in touch with the Godhead. Going to the source of the lie, or shadow, is a moral issue, and the resultant transformation is an alchemical act of ethical healing.

Zoja extends this kind of ethical investigation to the first psychoanalytical cases (Anna O. and Sabine Spielrein[10]) described by Freud and Jung. In his thorough examination of these original cases he uncovers unethical behavior in the reporting of what actually happened. Zoja uses a both/and combination of the old ethic, anchored to rules and law, and balances it with the new ethic, based on contact with an innate spiritual principle beyond the ego. He applies a "gray zone" ethical perspective to the initial cases of Sabine S. and Anna O. The result is an appreciation of the complex yet healing nature of being in analysis.

Zoja also delineates a new ethical frontier and helps us become aware of unethical issues involved in nonpersonal extensions of therapy and analysis involving computers, marketing, advertising, publications, and workshops. In addition, he focuses on the need for Ethics Committees to become more like Truth and Reconciliation panels involved in compassion, forgiveness, and healing.

Echoing the value of this perspective, I provide an actual example. Shortly after Zoja's Fay Lecture Series on Ethics and Analysis, I attended an annual meeting of the Inter-Regional Society of Jungian Analysts, which is a professional organization to which I belong. It was at this meeting that I encountered a moment of synchronicity, as an Appeals Committee reported a case that utilized the principles that Luigi Zoja had outlined. In response to ethical violations involving sexual transgression by a male analyst with several female patients, the Executive Committee of our professional Society set up a special Appeals Committee to monitor guidelines for a five-year probation, which, if met, would end his probation and allow the analyst to again be a member in good standing. The analyst admitted his unethical behavior, agreed to see no female patients, continued treatment with a Freudian analyst, had progress reports from weekly supervision sent to the Appeals Committee, and met with this Committee on a regular basis at biannual meetings of the Society. The analyst completed all the required tasks and made progress in getting to the source of his unethical behavior. Our Society had found a "gray zone" that allowed us to practice what we preached. I'll never forget the analyst standing before the whole society and saying, "I am grateful for the Appeals Committee's report. It has been a long five years, and I have thought of what I might say today. First of all, I would like to thank the Appeals Committee for your dedication in working with me and for the risk you took in acting favorably upon my appeal. I am well aware that my unethical behavior precipitated a painful ordeal for the Society and damaged several of my patients as well as myself. Being on probation, which I believe is unprecedented in the Inter-Regional, is a new dimension of our Society—one that has been most beneficial to me personally in allowing time and further analysis to uncover a shadow of which I was unconscious. During this period I have reflected upon my place, one might say in the 'space' I have occupied during probation. I have been, as it were, inside the Society yet outside it, participating yet not participating. Often in this space I felt a silent dialogue going on—perhaps unconsciously—between Society members and me. Many times I wondered how I might appear to the rest of the Society. I imagined, as I struggled with my shadow, that the Society struggled with its shadow, which, materialized in me, was now before you."[11]

This analyst's ordeal has renewed my faith in the new ethic proposed by Erich Neumann, and I close with a quote by him: "Modern man has lost his way; but the road which brings salvation to him is a road which leads downwards to a reunion with the unconscious, with the instinctual world of nature and with the ancestors, whose messenger is the shadow. He it is who brings the 'good news' of the treasure hidden in the depths, of the herb of healing which grows in the darkness and whose secret power is able to staunch the Amfortas-wound of modern man."[12]

Zoja ends his book on a very positive note, *Stil Novo*, in which he sees the therapeutic relationship as one of *temenos*, that is, sacred space. The transference/countertransference dynamic fully respects boundaries in an ethical sense, yet transcends them in our daily encounter to contain the opposites of good and evil and facilitate new beginnings and meanings in the context of a gentle, safe, and unique therapeutic relationship. In a real sense, this book is about an alchemy of ethics. It heralds the importance of containing and transforming the shadow. It is out of the gray that gold emerges.

Notes

1. Primo Levi, *The Damned and the Saved* (New York: Vintage, 1988).
2. Erich Neumann, *Depth Psychology and a New Ethic* (New York: G. P. Putnam's Sons, 1969).
3. Ibid., 147.
4. Available at http://www.supremecourtus.gov/about/figuresofjustice.pdf, accessed May 19, 2006.
5. Carol Gilligan, *In a Different Voice* (Cambridge, MA: Harvard University Press, 1982).
6. Available at http://www.supremecourtus.gov/about/figuresofjustice.pdf.

7. Peter Rutter, *Sex in the Forbidden Zone: When Men in Power—Therapists, Doctors, Clergy, Teachers, and Others—Betray Women's Trust* (New York: J. P. Tarcher, 1989).

8. Martin Buber, *Good and Evil* (New York: Charles Scribner's Sons, 1952), 7.

9. Ibid., 9.

10. This is the same person who is often cited in English language texts as Sabina Spielrein.

11. Personal communication; quoted from "Response to Probation's End."

12. Neumann, *Depth Psychology and a New Ethic,* 144.

Prologue

Why ethics *and* analysis? My original intent was to provide lectures on ethics *in* analysis, and to a great extent that was indeed the main topic of the lectures I delivered at Texas A&M University in April 2005. However, in turning those lectures into a book, I worked more and more on the introductory portion, which ended up becoming the entire first half of the final manuscript. An introduction to ethics in analysis turned into several chapters concerned with the philosophy of ethics in general.

This change arose from no fancy of my own but rather from a common need. Indeed, as the reader will see, one chief disappointment awaiting those who want to study ethics in analysis and psychotherapy comes from the fact that, although many books address that question, they mostly deal with rules. Ethics, on the contrary, is concerned with values and principles held in depth, a dimension into which specific, relative, and variable norms sink their roots. Such principles are tragically neglected in the existing literature, as if authors concerned with ethics in analysis were essentially concerned with ensuring punishment rather than with developing reflections on good and evil, principled reflections that might eventually lead to punishment or might not. This propensity on their part strikes me as being, so to speak, rather unethical, or at least unpsychological. Therefore, I felt that a general discussion of ethics was not only fitting but also necessary and long overdue in the context of analytic practice. It now constitutes the first part of the book, which is organically linked to the second, more specialist half.

In this second part, the reader will find that my references to analysis and psychotherapy alternate freely. For our purposes, in reflecting on the ethical dimensions of practice, we may treat these two branches of practice as being equivalent. Following the traditional definition of analysis, I consider analysis to stand as both the historical origin of psychotherapy and its in-depth form to this day, dealing as it does with both conscious and unconscious motivations and phenomena. Besides, the public attending the Fay Lectures was clearly acquainted with Jungian analysis, and I am a Jungian analyst myself. More to the point, the ethical implications of practice for practically all kinds of psychotherapy will not differ in kind from those found in analysis, apart from the fact that probably they tend to be expressed in milder forms. Ethics *and* analysis, ethics *and* psychotherapy: a distinction with a familial, harmonious difference.

Acknowledgments

I wish to thank the following persons for their roles in supporting both the original lectures and the book that has grown out of them.

First of all, my thanks to Carolyn Fay, whom I have proudly nominated and confirmed as Honorary Member of the Association for Analytical Psychology, and whose generosity has made many cultural initiatives possible, including my own lectures.

Then thanks to my editor John Peck, who has not only tuned my Italian English but also has served as a faithful and creatively dialectical counterpart. His efforts have stimulated new thinking and helped transform the rough notes of my Fay Lectures into a book.

Finally, my gratitude goes to Professor David Rosen, the extremely friendly host of an Italian lecturer otherwise lost in Texan immensity, and a demanding, professional, and reliable coeditor.

Part One

ETHICS:

ETHICS AS THE

ELABORATION OF COMPLEXITY

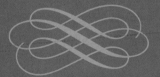

CHAPTER 1

Justice

One feature that distinguishes us as humans from other animals is that we want to know what is right and what is wrong. This deeply rooted desire has a unifying consequence for human inquiry and knowledge: all humanistic studies are transversely linked by ethics.

Taken one by one, the perspectives of philosophy, theology, psychology, sociology, or anthropology are "optional." We can, for instance, choose to look at human existence from a theological perspective, but we can also declare that we are secular and have no interest in it. Looking at things from the perspective of ethics, however, is inescapable; the right and wrong of a given situation chooses us, as we sooner or later discover from experience. We cannot simply declare that we are not interested in the distinction between right and wrong.

Since Aristotle ethics has been the study of good, and therefore also of goodness.[1] Its goal is an absolute and philosophical one, which includes all other goals as relative. Through the millennial authority of Aristotle, confirmed and spread by thinkers like Diogenes Laertius, the primacy of ethics has remained a constant feature of Western culture.

Immanuel Kant refined the study of ethics for modern philosophy by condensing our longing for justice into two ethical imperatives: the *categorical imperative* recommends following only those principles that we would establish as universal rules, while the *practical imperative* asks us always to consider the human being as a goal or end in itself, and never as an instrument or means.[2]

Since the Enlightenment of the European eighteenth century, we have lived in an essentially secular world. Toward the end of that century, the American and French Revolutions irreversibly posited a separation between the authorities of Church and State. Toward the end of the nineteenth century, following Nietzsche's famous posting of a death notice for the traditional conception of God, humankind has been increasingly left alone in deciding what ethics is, and in determining what is right and wrong.

Left alone, yet also of necessity more urgently grounded in the enterprise, Carl Gustav Jung has adhered to the tradition that assumes that ethics is central to every discipline.[3] And he specifically claimed that deep psychotherapeutic healing is an ethical act, and that every ethical act is indirectly therapeutic. Nor has Jung been alone in placing ethical activity at the center of modern humanity's task. The whole teaching of Levinas, explicitly or implicitly, consists of ethical reflection. In turn, Zygmunt Bauman has rooted the centrality of ethics in sociology, stating that while after the horrors of the twentieth century traditional ethical codes have lost their relevance, still in every society a deep, prerational longing for ethics has become more central than ever.[4]

Yet Jung's psychology occupies a unique position in any such array. Erich Neumann—a Jew from Berlin who immigrated to Israel after having analyzed with Jung—was probably the first to understand that depth psychology, and specifically Jungian psychology, were not exclusively therapeutic, but also constituted an enormous cultural and moral revolution. This contribution had arrived, Neumann noted, during a peculiar acceleration of urgencies. At the end of World War II he observed that the world had hardly time to know itself as liberated from the threat of Nazism because the liberators were already threatening each other, and the fate of life on earth, with nuclear weapons. With this unique historical threat, however, also comes a unique opportunity. Neumann accordingly attempted to turn Jungian psychology into the basis for new ethics.[5] Traditional Judeo-Christian ethics have offered a basis for understandable and relatively functional moral rules governing both human behavior and attributions of responsibility. However, this ethical dispensation has taken pride of place at enormous cost to individual ethical awareness. General rules have been privileged. Individual understanding and individual authority based on that understanding have been accepted only as the wards of toleration or as remarkable, sometimes freakish, exceptions. The issue of guilt has been simplified, tending toward attributions that assign the moral burden to only one of two polarities. Collective attributions of responsibility coexist with individual ones, with the consequence that punishment can also be made collective. Psychological dynamics are denied wholesale, with the result that they take place unconsciously: the guilt of the other party is regularly overstated because one's own guilt is denied and projected onto the counterpart.

To overcome this "old ethics," as Neumann calls it, becomes in itself a considerable moral task, and with enormous stakes for survival, because the persistence of traditional ethical guidelines entails the risk that they will turn mutual attributions of guilt into collective paranoia, as both hot and cold wars have shown, in an era when there will be little or no margin for error. Neumann proposes "new ethics" as the best way through the impasse of projection left by the older set. A psychological perspective must guide the new ethics for our situation. Ethical evaluation should start with introspection and analysis of one's own "shadow side," thereby leading gradually to an integration of the "inner opposite polarity."[6] Such ethics will necessarily be individually oriented, less punitive than the traditional ones, and will remain focused on positive, educational goals—on the growth of consciousness in the place where it happens first, in the individual.

The relationship between ethics and religion has been a changing one. Ancient polytheism displayed gods who had little or nothing to do with justice. On the one hand, the God of the Old Testament can be less moral than His creatures, as Job's torments remind us. On the other hand, modernity, having developed rationality, allows God to survive provided that He collaborates in the search for a rational and functional justice.

If we believe in God, we call Him the Creator. And indeed, only divine creativity could invent a being as capable of injustice as man. But

God also loves complexity and paradoxes, and so He endowed His perverted creature with a permanent longing for justice. The longing for this divine (or, depending on the perspective, archetypal) quality seems even stronger than the longing for God Himself. It survives secularization and atheism. Actually, it seems that secularization and atheism reinforce our need for justice. *Once God isn't any more the direct administrator of justice, we inherit his responsibility. We can do without Him, but not without the principle of justice,* which is His most inescapable legacy.

This is comforting and, at the same time, frightening. Comforting, because our secular society has retained the moral core of religious teaching. Frightening, because in pursuing justice we humans unconsciously enact God's role.

We tend to overlook the dramatic implications of this enactment for the human psyche. When we read Hitler's or Stalin's statements about justice, we dismiss them as expressions of immorality. The tragic truth is that these men were sincere in making such statements. The main problem with them was psychological, not political. As Neumann would put it, that problem was a lack in elaborating the shadow.[7]

A liar knows that he might, one day or another, be discovered, and if so that he will be sanctioned. He knows that he is up against boundaries, and so such a normal liar is human. Most tyrants, on the contrary, possessing a power that is formally limitless, identify with a divine archetype. Even in our own day they enact the principle that legitimized absolute authority in the predemocratic state and was minted for thousands of years on most coins: *Dei Gratia* (out of God's personal concession). Archetypes erase history and connect one directly with the original psychological source: in this case, with God, who was supposed to be the direct source of every political power. A tyrant cannot even imagine that he might be accountable to a system of justice. He IS direct divine justice.

*L*et me frame three brief theses about justice.

First, we do not pursue justice because we have an *interest* in it. We pursue it because we experience it as a *necessity.*

Second, not only is justice an archetypal necessity, it also claims the right to subordinate all other archetypal drives to its control.

And third, in the idea of justice the essence of religion is preserved in secular terms. As in the case of religion, justice is endowed with an absolute, totalizing quality. Yet justice is the senior partner, for in many respects this quality on its own ends up being more absolute than it is in religion.

Before turning Christian, what was considered the most civilized part of Europe was ruled by Greco-Roman polytheism. As already noted, this religion with many gods in a certain sense had an aesthetic more than an ethical function. The gods existed so that it would be possible to tell amazing tales about them. Their existence served literary more than theological or moral purposes. Therefore the idea of justice lived its separate, somehow precociously secular existence. Humans cared about it more than the gods did, and felt themselves, in this respect, to be tragically alone. Their only, but essential, rule was modesty: do not try to imitate the gods, avoid arrogance, and practice self-limitation. One of the two rules at the sanctuary of Delphi was: "nothing [should be] too much."[8]

From Socrates on, certain thinkers dedicated their efforts to the formulation of justice, and were called philosophers. But justice was already present before those attempts to formulate it in rational terms. Being as yet undefined, it did not translate into rules and codes. It could be the latent content of a tale, and could also be offered to the whole of a society as an aesthetic experience through drama.

The most powerful ancient instance known to us is Sophocles' play *Antigone*, which is centered on the eternal opposition between justice and law. Antigone refuses to obey a law forbidding the burial of her brother Polynix. The law is relative: viewing Polynix as a traitor, the king wants to carry out an exemplary humiliation of his body. Antigone claims though that justice is absolute and eternal, and that justice requires respect both for relatives and for all the dead, along with their ritual burial.

A radical longing for justice by the individual is no invention of modern democracies. The fact that *Antigone* is possibly the most famous of ancient dramas reminds us that, even two and a half millennia ago, the audience fully agreed with the idea that an ordinary citizen could know justice better than the king, and a woman better than a man. The awareness of justice is, was, and should remain more important than knowledge of and respect for the law.

In one respect laws are standardized and impersonal, but in another they change with time and place. Justice corresponds, in one perspective, to an eternal, archetypal drive, but in another it shows up in personalized forms. The relativism of so-called positive law—specific legislation and all its related judicial findings—only does what it can (or perhaps holds back from doing what it can) to represent archetypal justice. Justice (which might include unconscious psychological elements, thus corresponding to what Neumann calls "new ethics") is therefore more important than law.[9] This perspective on justice and law, as we know, prevailed not only in ancient Greece. The largest and oldest civilization on earth—China—has thrived until today by letting its courts rule not on the basis of codes but of traditions that public sentiment considers just.

Following these premises, we would do best to stick to the traditional meaning of ethics. My discussion, taking its orientation from archetypal promptings, wants to participate in the universal longing for justice, rather than offering one more attempt to codify rules and laws.

CHAPTER 2

Beauty

The religious, and therefore to a great extent, the cultural roots of the Western world are, on the one hand, Jewish monotheism, and on the other Greek polytheism. But the values inspiring Jewish monotheism are ethical, while those supporting Greek polytheism were, to a great extent, aesthetic.

For the modern mentality, with its abstract and defining categories, the contraposition between ethics and aesthetics is clear. Aesthetics can remain personal and relative; ethics inherently strives toward the absolute. Therefore we can do without aesthetics but cannot escape ethics. The Greeks, to whom we owe the *definitions* of both ethics and aesthetics, would have rejected their *separation*. There were no written codes that defined beauty or goodness. But there was a general consensus about both, and also a consensus about the fact that they belong together. The two were different expressions of the same quality—excellence—to such an extent that their kinship came to be expressed by combining the two words in one: *kalokagathia* = beauty-and-goodness. Both corresponded to the longing for something divine. Yes, one could describe them, in the manner of an abstract exercise, as two distinct things. But in concrete reality it was assumed that they always came together—as two faces of the same coin—because the longing that animates them, the soul's search for elevation, is inherently one. In the sense proposed by Martin Buber, these two ideas were *Grundworte* (basic words): concepts that perform their function only if related as a dyad, never alone.[1]

Instrumental functionalism has gradually separated these two supreme qualities, to the loss of aesthetics. The complexity of our society requires increasingly specific roles with exactly delimited functions, and therefore a constant definition, in terms of performance, of what is right and wrong. For a well-functioning society, ethics are a necessity, but chiefly in this reductive sense of a set of rules. The same complexity tends to abolish beauty as a supreme value, because it encroaches on the new "values" of efficiency, speed, and economic measurement. Aesthetic priorities, too bad for them, tend to be anti-functional and anti-economical.

Why have we lost hold of the unitary idea that goodness and beauty go together? As we have recalled, our need to be just tends to be felt as an original, natural impulse, which precedes rational calculation. In a similar way, we experience a natural desire for beauty. The aspirations to goodness and beauty are so similar that to prefer ugliness to beauty can be sensed inwardly as an "evil intention."

No Greek temple has ever offended a landscape, although all of them were built where nowadays no license to build would be granted. The same ought to be said of Greek theaters, huge for their time, which exploited already existing slopes. Yet those who commission modern architecture would just as happily build shopping centers in the same places. A Greek theater collaborates with the landscape, using it by closely relating itself to it, whereas a shopping mall abuses it by violently intruding into an existing harmony.[2] *In its concrete and original expression*—before becoming mannerism, kitsch, conspicuous consumption, or anti-aesthetic exhibitionism—*aesthetics aims at fighting abuse no less than ethics does.* At the very least, then, we have lost hold of the original unitary idea because we no longer allow beauty to put up its own kind of fight.

And we no longer *see* beauty act integrally. We have come to consider attending the theater as an entertainment, like going to the cinema or watching TV. Nothing could be more inappropriate, indeed wrong. This behavior is like equating religious objects (for instance, an ancient golden cross meant for rituals) to treasury bonds or shares of stock, because certain collectors have transformed them into investments. Theater was a religious experience (its etymon is the same as in *theòs*, God). The entire population attended. Through deep and common emotion, Greek theater performed a ritual in honor of the god Dionysus. This ritual, at the same time, divinized the *polis* (the ancient Greek city-state) and the sentiments of equality and of mutual belonging it gave to all citizens.[3] It was simply impossible to separate the religious experience from the mundane pleasure of watching a performance (which of course was also there!), or the personal from the collective (from another perspective: the psychological from the sociological), or the aesthetic from the ethical.

All this co-inherence was a powerful factor in making that society into the one that we still envy: constantly engaged in cultural life provided at no cost; driven toward common goals without waiting to be compelled (the wealthy, for instance, competed in paying for endeavors of common interest, because they considered it an honor); capable of staggeringly precocious scientific inventions; almost untouched by organized crime; and ready, if necessary, to take up arms and defeat much larger armies of professional soldiers.[4]

Commercial, cultural, and political activity tended to be promoted and elaborated in daily contacts in the public square, the agora. This term not only designates a place—like the English word "square" or, not by chance, the French *place*—but also implies an action: the verb *ageíro* means to gather.

European history offers a simulacrum of sorts for the great Greek ingathering. For in the Italian city-states of the late Middle Ages and early Renaissance, public life consistently nourished beauty and aesthetic—not only ethical—balance. The community was small; the unwritten rules of social control still functioned. For a fragile period, even the duality of Church and State remained balanced and seemed to form a necessary complementarity, as do the faces on a coin. In the main square, or *piazza*, the communal palace, or *palazzo*, rose beside the cathedral, or *duomo*. The heights of these respective towers identified a symbolic and potentially explosive issue. The increasingly secular political power rivaled (at least as long as it did not turn tyrannical) the religious one in offering its citizens not only the highest tower but often, also, the highest caliber of art.

A paradox concerning the Church of that age is often forgotten. While the Church of Rome was then probably at the height of its corruption, in this sense reaching the lowest ethical level ever achieved by a religious institution (not by coincidence, those times ended with the West's most profound religious rebellion, the Reformation), even so the Church, as a cultural institution, served an exceptional function. As with the Greek theater but reversing the ratio, going to church was not only a religious but also a totalizing humanistic experience. Even poor and uneducated citizens shared a fusional ritual of belonging to a collective, to its values, goals, and citizenship. They participated in a liturgy that made use of the most precious jewels, listened to elevated music, and perhaps glimpsed the finest painting of the era. All this was manifest to them at no personal cost. In a certain sense, the Church had probably lost God without losing the soul. For the soul is also culture; it is also an elevated, and elevating, experience of beauty.

On the other side of the coin, the Empire rivaled the Church in jockeying for absolute power over Europe (or at least over its historical kernel: not incidentally it asserted its claim to be the heir of its Roman prototype) and was prone to use the same instruments. Art was the mass medium of those times, and both the popes and the emperors, out of sheer political calculation, end up deserving major historical credit for favoring the arts. To name but one emperor: Frederick I Barbarossa was an unsurpassed builder of churches, a patron of the arts and sciences, and also, in his relentless curiosity and cynicism, a precursor of modern man. Under his supervision, new techniques and art forms received support. While it was impossible to magnify sculptural scale indefinitely, the new techniques of fresco lent enormous visibility to public art, becoming the ideal instrument for turning the insides of churches and public buildings into platforms for propaganda.[5]

CHAPTER 3

Palace and Square

Since we are speaking of the Italian Renaissance, let us detour through an important idea (actually, two ideas combined into several polarities, again along the lines of Jung's archetype or of Buber's *Grundworte*) as it was employed by one of that era's most prominent writers.

Niccoló Machiavelli, still considered the father of political science, is not content with superficial accounts of events in his *Florentine History*, written in 1525, but delves deeply into the factors that caused Florence's decline and loss of influence after leading the Western world out of the Middle Ages and serving as its cultural capital. In particular he examines the exercise of political power, which had become arrogant and autocratic, calling it the *palagio* (palace, from the Roman hill *palatinum* where the imperial palace or *palatium* stood).[1] And he calls the disaffected, excluded community of citizens—at times, in a more negative undertone, the populace or the mob—the *piazza* (from the Latin *platea*, in turn from the Greek *plateia*, both meaning large road or square: an adjective made into a noun). The meaning of *piazza* closely resembles that of agora, therefore indicating not only a physical place but also implying the intention of actively gathering there. It also suggests something done regularly, or daily, in the manner of a social right or duty (cf. the French *trouver une place*, to find a job).

As a part of urban reality, the derivatives of *piazza* have survived in the main Western languages, except in English, where the notion indicates a space in general, or a quality connected with reality; for example, "it has taken place," meaning that it has happened. Of course, the English language employs "square" as its standard equivalent for the Greek/Latin "place." But this describes only a *space* in the city. When in English one refers not only to public ground but also to the mob or to civil society expressing its will in that space, one says "the street" (for instance, "the street has imposed its will on the governor").

The difference is quite significant. English has attained preeminence with the dominant influence of the New World, both geopolitically and in the sense of the Modern Age. The urbanism of the new world is chiefly a matter of streets rather than squares. Of course, squares are built too, but as accessories of the streets, whereas the reverse was the case in both the Greek *polis* and the city-states of the Italian Renaissance. Modern towns serve a population that needs public space in order to move from one address to another, not in order to gather and do essential common business in the open.

Therefore, straight lines dominate over curves (just as fascism also had it, considering straight lines more masculine and using them to dominate the femininity of the art deco and liberty styles). Intelligent architects take note of such one-sidedness and work against it. The Chrysler Building bravely combined curves and straight lines, and the groundbreaking Austrian painter and architect Hundertwasser declared that "the straight line is Godless" while laying out floors with camel-like undulations.[2] But at the end of the day, when the overall functionalism of the structure has won out, such expressions of good will show themselves to be the late-applied rouge and silicone breasts that they are.

I have invited you to follow the ancient, archetypal distinction between *piazza* and *palazzo* to let me underscore a dramatic feature of Western history, which has an important bearing on ethics. This feature has two aspects—first, that throughout history the *piazza* has been fading out (that is to say, the Old World has gradually submitted to New World town planning), and second, that the *piazza*—intended as shared communal life—was essential not only to more manageable politics but also to the experience of beauty. The disappearance of a shared aesthetic experience through the disappearance of common space and its activity of communal gathering is a decisive factor behind the growing ethical problems of modern society.

It is clear that no one can claim that the average ancient Greek or Renaissance Italian citizen was assured of always having access to the finest sculptures, the best theater, the most impressive cathedrals, and the choicest paintings. As at any other time in history, people in those societies could be gross and insensitive. At the same time, however, what Jung calls the collective psyche was constantly nourished by the ratio we have been laying out between the elements in an archetypal dyad—by beauty and an ideal of beauty that were indistinguishable from the ideal of justice.

This nourishment by an archetypal polarity in balance, together with the relatively contained scale of those societies, probably kept them both more manageable and less prone to violence, and the individuals within them psychologically more stable. This is not to say that Greek and Renaissance cities were free of murder and theft, but to propose that under those circumstances—for instance in the unquenchable individualism of the Renaissance—violence tended to be a personal expression; it was, so to speak, the shadow side of an often spectacular and creative individual fantasy.[3] It did not translate, as it does today, into organized mafia operations or colossal economic criminality, whose staggering scale and impact presuppose immense areas of collusion in the society—a structural poisoning of the collective psyche, not the occasional poisoning of certain individuals.

Comparable examples of balanced life in today's world have become extremely rare. One such noteworthy example—until the very recent and corrupting explosion of Western mass tourism—is the small island of Bali, which throughout the first part of the second millennium attracted several waves of immigration by the cultivated classes and court artists from Java and other surrounding islands, who fled the advance of Islam. As a result, it maintained a tradition of religious toleration and aesthetic richness. Significantly in Bali, large amounts of time, energy, and money traditionally have been devoted—through a collective dedication by the entire population—to rituals that afford great beauty; and Bali, probably not by accident, has consistently enjoyed the relative absence of organized crime.

Today, in the affluent West, our masses are relatively well off, enjoying *wide access to commodities* (cars, home appliances) and almost *unlimited access to entertainment* (TV, the Internet). But they have been *denied access to beauty.* In view of the archetypal balance that we have collectively lost, between the energies of justice and beauty, or ethics and aesthetics, the suspicion should arise that this comprehensive fact about our common life plays a role in the diffusion of senseless unethical behavior. We hear on every side that the masses have no values, no ideals. The implication is that we can answer such outcries with moral remedies already at hand. Yet is it possible to teach ideals of justice without ideals of beauty, and respect for ethical values without respect for aesthetic ones? Indeed, the impression grows that in the most daunting moral issues—like the protection of the environment and the prospects of life for any number of species—we face a task that is indistinguishably ethical and aesthetic.

Along with such realizations comes the awareness that the greater part of the population, by substituting entertainment for beauty, has not been treading a neutral path. It has traded something invaluable for something ethically dangerous; almost daily, entertainment and so-called news programming display violence, render us accustomed to violence, an-aesthetize us in the immediate presence of violence, and teach us violence.[4]

Beauty, on the contrary, works against such inner disturbance. Because it speaks to more than the specific time and place where it has been produced, it touches eternal, absolute value, reminding those who live with it that they can experience something sublime through simple contemplation. It induces calm, making aggressiveness and striving irrelevant. And by virtue of the respect for beauty that grows from such experience, the control of our destructive drives may cease to be such an effort and actually become more instinctive.

Real beauty, whether classical or otherwise, has something of the folktale quality of being inexhaustible. Unlike reserves of food and the serial installments of entertainment, beauty does not diminish. It can abide as a source, nourishing countless numbers of people over an indefinite time. It remains durably outside even as one incorporates an essential part of it, like the self-renewing folktale meal with self-replenishing wine. Leonardo da Vinci's fresco of the *Last Supper* in Milan, in spite of decay resulting from his experimental techniques, really is a supper that lasts, nourishing countless visitors over the centuries. With such inherent and paradoxical abundance, beauty teaches the irrelevance of greed and of continuous appropriation. One can be content with it, and with oneself as well, without any need to turn psychologically obese.

Only if one actually knows what beauty is from experience can one truly perceive the actual force of contemporary injustice. Typical examples of modern mass criminality are also archetypical in their impact—such as illegal construction or illegal deforestation—because as egoistic appropriation and destruction of the common good they offend ethics and aesthetics at the same, indistinguishable time (and for which the Italian official term, not by chance, is *abuso*).

Correspondingly, only through the experience of beauty can one properly estimate the deficiencies of modern justice. In present-day mass society, the rule of law is often carried out, not in balanced relation to the rule of beauty but with the misrule of ugliness. Indeed, the ordinary citizen is frequently deprived of the very idea of balance. The preference for balanced as opposed to unbalanced perceptions is an instinctive aesthetic need. The dry rule of modern legal practice—deprived of the "rule of balances"—often imposes itself by means of sheer rationality, as something convenient—that is, a convening of precedents and rights without reference to sustaining support from the cultivated instinct we have been tracking: a convening that lacks balanced gathering. Traditional, archetypal iconography with good reason always associated crime with ugliness. Ugliness was therefore instinctively avoided as "horrible" (an adjective that expressed immediate rejection of something archetypically "wrong: loathsome and fearful, without distinction"; the Latin verb *horreo* literally indicated the rising of hair on the skin). Today, crime has retreated from the horrible to a prevailingly neutral zone, an an-aesthetic region in which criminal violation is rationally kept at a distance and waits upon a calculation of the corresponding sanctions.

It has been said that TV—being one of the few modern ritual occasions for gathering—constitutes the new *piazza*. Nothing could be more false. TV is the *palazzo* in its pure state, at the apex of its arrogance. TV is the *palazzo* speaking to what was once the *piazza* in a one-sided way. It used to be that if the *piazza* got fed up it could throw rotten eggs at the *palazzo*, or even set fire to it. Today, the former *piazza*-turned-audience can only swallow visual junk food—the modern equivalent of rotten eggs—or unplug.

The *piazza* as the basis for the "public thing" or *res publica*, the shared experience, has truly disappeared. And with it has gone any sustained access to a common education by beauty, which for centuries helped to render the human soul as more gentle. Mass reproduction, as philosopher Walter Benjamin urgently pointed out, is no substitute for what has vanished, which amounts to nothing less than a more complete way of experiencing the world. And, in our terms here, a way that is archetypally sound and sane, *sanum*, healthy. We are not dealing with what advertisers call "appreciation." It used to be that an ordinary citizen could routinely spend time in the presence of paintings by Michelangelo or Raphael or Rosso Fiorentino, as a part of his everyday experience. Today, only a wealthy billionaire can buy a Michelangelo and hang it in his private collection. Of course, there are also museums; and of course many billionaires allow public access to their collections. That, however, does not give us back the *piazza*: it simply opens a back door in the *palazzo*. How often does the man-in-the-street switch off his television to go to the museum? He can miss Michelangelo for the whole of his life, but he will never miss the last installment of his serial.

Nor does modern art seem to offer a solution, for it gives us back not classical, "absolute" beauty but something else. It often rather increases the problem. With modern art, the split between audiences grows until it becomes irreversible. Not only is the work of art enclosed in a *palazzo* (called the museum), which intimidates the uneducated as something elitist, but modern works of art are also experienced—Picasso or Warhol in painting, Moore in sculpture, Schoenberg in music—within brackets, like winks tipped between intellectuals, requiring quite a high level of education for their understanding and enjoyment. Not by chance, art has come to be self-referential. Pirandello writes plays about writing plays. Magritte produces paintings about the concept of painting. Truffaut and Fellini make films about making films, and Gide writes about writing—and so on. This art implies the art critic as traditional religion has implied the priest.

It was not always so. Once, the entire population of Athens—wealthy or poor, refined or gross—together witnessed whole cycles of dramatic performance, and was moved as one community by the sublime simplicity of Aeschylus or Sophocles. Today, the beholding of performance follows an implicit apartheid: here, intellectual shows for a select minority; there, mass entertainment as nourishing as chewing gum. This demographic separation mimics the more profound separation between our ethics and our aesthetics (or an-aesthetics), between our jointly exiled senses of the just and the good. We can see how we got there, but even so, in mutual astonishment, we must still ask: how did we reach this point? How is it possible that Western society—which undoubtedly has become wealthier and more democratic—has been so arrogant in denying beauty to the majority of its population?

CHAPTER 4

Can Evil Be Avoided
If Ugliness Is Compulsory?

Ethical values have been debated more and more thoroughly through the course of history. As we have argued, this debate is *functional* to a modern society. Politics requires growing connections with ethics. The diffusion of democracy and transparency constantly puts politicians to task. Not only must they claim that they represent good against evil, but they are also asked to prove it by respecting acknowledged standards. Also, because the importance of economics has grown exponentially, economics, and its ethical implications, continually require new agreements about what is right and what is wrong (we shall return to this).

The downside of this positive development is that ethics is not directly promoted by a moral drive, but indirectly or even incidentally by a utilitarian thrust toward better functioning. New standards and rules receive attention and win favor, rather than new ethics or a deeper sense of justice.

Being herded down that functional path, ethical values have gradually lost connection with aesthetic ones. Aesthetics is necessary neither for economic functioning (capitalism requires rules—which claim to represent some justice—but not beauty) nor for political life (numerous crusades are mounted by good against evil, but hardly any by beauty against ugliness).

The history of the link between ethics and aesthetics is related to the history of religion.

In its attempt to extend its spiritual power throughout the immense ecumene of the Roman Empire, the Church merged the new culture of Christianity with the existing culture's mythology, its penchant for images, and its appetite for the entire aesthetic amalgam of experience that we call Mediterranean. Thereby the Church deposited in the cellar of the new religion an unexpressed but solid base of Greco-Roman paganism (a fact that Jung often praises).

After the corruption and various excesses of power within the Roman Church had gradually led to internal revolts and finally to the Reformation, the Catholic Church had to go on the defensive, entrenching itself in its Mediterranean stronghold. Its apparently successful export to Latin America was partly due to fortuitous historical circumstances, as the present, growing conversions to Protestantism there seem to confirm. The New World—in the geographical but also in the historical sense of "more modern" world—has been successfully conquered by the Reformation, particularly by that branch that went farthest from Rome: Puritanism. That victory, as Max Weber convincingly argued a century ago, was to go hand in hand with the triumph of modern capitalistic society and its staggering production of wealth.[1] But this joint development also accelerated and strengthened a highly relevant factor that has been much less studied: the devaluation of aesthetic values.

With the Reformation, the Church went, so to say, back to God, not only as an institution but also as an edifice. It was meant for Him and for the spirit, not for the sensual enjoyment of paintings, music, incense, and ritual. In a certain way, this trend rejected the historical compromise with ancient polytheism brought about by the Roman Church. Instead, it reactivated the ban on human images already central in Judaism and Islam.

Puritan traditions, practicality, the avoidance of unnecessary decoration, a no-nonsense attitude, and an abhorrence of wasted time have assured that the American ideal of straightforward dedication to work, through military victories in two world wars and economic victory in the cold war and globalization, has been exported to every corner of the planet. This fact has indisputable advantages, just as it is indisputable that the Catholic Church deserved to be shaken and partly defeated by the Reformation. But all this was not without great cost. We may have thrown out a quite respectable baby with the bath water.

$\mathcal{R}$adical defeat of the Axis Powers was the only possible response to fascism. This central outcome has been so obviously desirable that very little analysis has been devoted to its further consequences. Yet every strong medicine has side effects, and every radical war produces collateral damages. Let us, then, examine one such cultural consequence of the Allied victory. The radical forms of nationalism known as fascism and Nazism were so hideous that, after the war, an instinctive reshaping of cultural identity in Europe became a self-evident necessity. As I have discussed on another occasion, the idea of nationalism and the adjective "national" all but disappeared.[2] The new generations in Italy and Germany have turned to McDonalds and blue jeans with more enthusiasm than have the parallel generations in America, and for a while they adopted revolutionary ideas with more élan than the (by then conservative) Soviet Union. Although at a slower pace, something similar has also taken place in Japan.

These postwar generations not only felt *allowed* to turn their backs on their parents (a temptation common to all times) along with their national cultures, but they also felt, probably for the first time in history, morally *obliged* to do so. Incidentally but also momentously, this strong and, to a great extent, unconscious identification with the Allies planted a potent seed of the globalization to come.

The parents were incapable of pulling the youth back into line, but that was not all. Understandably, newly emerging commercial classes also favored the movement. In the fervor of reconstruction, mass production of new goods was quick to take root, and the American way of life was pursued with no consideration for the fact that American mass wealth was the result of long generational processes, set in motion by the Founding Fathers and historically tied to a particular set of liberties—in short, that American affluence meant the preservation of an "American soul" or national culture. In the former Axis countries, on the contrary, the adoption of such lifeways corresponded in no small degree to the demise of their national souls.

Let us not forget that in Italy, after fascism (and also before that among the working class to a large extent), there was hardly any identification with the national state that could go by the name of national culture, in contrast to American collective consciousness, which correctly has been called "civil religion." The national culture of Italy used to be historically connected with the culture of the Renaissance and its aesthetic tradition. That heritage is particularly powerful, inasmuch as the Renaissance exerts an overwhelming dominance in comparison to all other aspects of cultural inheritance: because of this factor's peculiar weighting, UNESCO reckons that between 40 and 50 percent of all art treasures worldwide are located in Italy.

Something quite similar happened in Germany. There, too, national culture corresponded only minimally with the modern national state (the dictatorship provoked strong identification but did not last long, and is now seen by Germans as a unique, historically confined pathology). The most powerful backbone of Germany's national culture was romanticism. For our purposes, we can regard it as a deeply aesthetic reaction to the Enlightenment, which was perceived as a movement that risked turning modern culture into something too rational.

As for the case of Japan, and even taking into account the difficulties of comparing Asian with Western culture, we should remember that the traditional aesthetics of Japan was a coupling of elegance with sobriety. Its partial repression after World War II corresponded not incidentally to Japan's highly successful turn to the hectic completion of its modernization through industrial mass production that, by its very nature, demands that one ignore sobriety.

So, in the three Axis powers defeated in World War II, the denial of national cultures ended up corresponding, in very large part, to a *denial of traditional aesthetics.*

The polarization between democracy and the Axis resulted in the suppression of one pole in the tension. This is hardly to be regretted: the Axis represented a virulently infectious strain of modern nationalism, not one more cultural step gradually leading somewhere. Its defeat, however, resulted in a sudden, drastic attempt to repress three rich national cultural traditions. With respect to the archetypal dyad of ethics versus aesthetics, we can see that older aesthetic cultural traditions were suppressed by the no-nonsense ethos of the Anglo-Saxon Allies, especially its American aspect. This was the second conquest as it were, carried out from within through an artificial, accelerated conversion to modernization and to aesthetic modernism by Italy, Germany, and Japan.

The second half of the twentieth century has witnessed the second radical world victory of the West, with the defeat of communism by commercial competition. Karl Marx had proposed a project that, from the perspective of our theme, amounts to an ethical re-orientation of economics. His goal of radical justice among social classes has proved unviable. Not only was justice scarcely achieved in formally communist societies, but also the revolutionary restructuring of society proved either to be impossible, or possible only at such high cost in violence that it turned itself into a new, dramatic injustice.

There is something in this failure, however, that is both relevant to our topic and, to my knowledge, has not been discussed.

It hinges upon aesthetics. Most fundamentally of all, perhaps, the communist project was radically unbalanced in its archetypal polarities. In its concrete, historical incarnations, either it ended up ignoring aesthetics or it proposed programmatic intellectual substitutes for them, like so-called socialist realism. Without denying the impressive swings and shifts in cultural fashion, the aesthetics running through and beneath them are deep, century-old streams that moisten and nourish the so-called collective unconscious. They can of course be renewed and accelerated by powerful new contributions, but never re-invented in a few years by intellectuals—let alone by party functionaries.

So, we ought to put the question to radical social programs on the profound basis of the ethical-aesthetic dyad itself: to what extent was the general disaffection for communism in Eastern Europe the result not only of deficient justice (an ethical miscarriage) but also of a radical aesthetic deficiency (a profound anemia of the cultural bloodlines in the countries swept into the Soviet bloc)? And another question follows: isn't a radically one-sided society—in this case concerned with ethics at the expense of aesthetics, preoccupied by justice but ignoring beauty—doomed to suffer a paradoxical reversal, an *enantiodromia*?[3] When that radical counterswing began among the countries of the Eastern bloc, and official justice stood unmasked as injustice, the immediate tendency afterward expressed a hysterical, egoistic craving for lost beauty. I have in mind here neither Havel's plays nor Brodsky's poems, which long preceded the counterswing, but rather an uneducated and unconscious reaction that showed up in mostly perverted forms, like the grotesquely conspicuous consumption of many Russian nouveau riches.

At any rate, what most postcommunist societies (among which China should be counted as well) are experiencing is a specific reaction, which probably will find its limits precisely because it follows a predictable cycle. What should concern us most lies beyond the range of unconscious dynamics of that kind, in the overall future balance of ethics and aesthetics in postmodern society.

Preeminent in that question of balance is ethical deformation. For example, it is possible that a society that has lost or repressed the aesthetic polarity ends up—in order to maintain its one-sided denial of the beautiful—leaning toward determinism and fundamentalism. Because it is concerned only with right versus wrong, and not also with the beautiful versus the ugly, it might assume missionary attitudes and be prone to religious wars. (There are, on the contrary, no wars due to aesthetic fundamentalism, although iconoclasm has played a role in some of them.) Such a society tends to deny the possibilities of both destiny and tragedy, which have been deeply rooted in aesthetic cultures (more about this later). And when destiny and tragedy strike— because sooner or later they do—it denies them as such and therefore needs to find scapegoats, in enemies either hidden or visible. In short, it projects the impacts of these realities because it sees them as inhuman. The perception of destiny and tragedy is indeed linked with aesthetic perception, and in our optimistic simplifications—which have comfort as their main aim—we deny them both.

Let us go back to our starting point. At least in our affluent West, starvation for food no longer seems relevant, and this has worked against Marx's prophecy. But, if we turn from food for the body to nourishment of the soul, what shall we say about being starved for beauty? This psychic misery has reached an all-time historic high. Not only is beauty disappearing from before our eyes, in eroded landscapes, functional and dull architecture, vanishing craft skill, mass production, and coterie art that restricts access, it is also the case that those who can afford beauty have reached an all-time low. While physical nourishment was once a challenge for manual workers, this famine of the soul is systemic, affecting not only what is left of the working class *and* the middle class, but even a major portion of the elites. We have gone from relatively small societies that rendered beauty accessible to everyone, to a global one that guarantees it to almost no one.

This is an unprecedented impoverishment of the human being, which cannot be compensated simply by having more cars or even by better healthcare. It is a historical injustice perpetrated against beauty itself, and against us who are more and more deprived of it. *If aesthetics suffer injustice, they become an ethical issue. Aesthetics deprived become ethics reborn.* We are back to the archetypal couple cultivated by the Greeks. Paradoxically, it is through sufferance of their separation and imbalance that we might begin to recover their unity.

CHAPTER 5

Has Beauty Been Shrinking throughout History?

Can we imagine beauty dying away once and for all?

Speaking of ethics, Neumann reminds us that it is precisely when Goliath seems to win that David conquers.[1]

At midnight noon is born, but what of a culture in which the sun seems never to have wholly set? People of other nationalities often tell Italians that aesthetics are so deeply embedded in Italian history that they cannot get lost. They often cite as their example the fact that Italy is still the leading country in fashion. Let us test their proposition, then, with a review of recent history.

That test reveals Italian supremacy in fashion to be anything but a reassurance. Before World War II, a proper aesthetic tradition was still active, although dwindling toward the status of a commodity. Italian ocean liners were renowned for their combination of sleek design, fine cuisine, interior decoration, and paintings. Directly after the war, the new, dominating forms of industrial society still welcomed the capacity to express a certain beauty. Although architecture, in the haste of postwar reconstruction, turned monstrous and deadly, Italian automobiles still showed captivatingly elegant lines: one of them was even put on show at the Museum of Modern Art in New York. Industrial necessity, however, soon withered even that charm, although elegance survived, taking a step away from the streets and public squares toward individualism: it took refuge in private spaces, crawling into the design of home appliances. But after only a short while such design too decayed, yielding to the exigencies of mass production. The longing for beauty thus made its final move, merging at last with egoism and narcissism, and the season of fashion blossomed.[2]

If a necessity is archetypal—as we assume that the need for beauty is—denial of it will result not in its disappearance but in its expression in unconscious, neurotic, perverted ways. The postwar, postfascist exposure to beauty gradually turned to hysterical and narcissistic forms.

When beauty was still valued as much as justice, it was mostly public (as justice had to be): both were manifest in the temple, the agora, the *piazza*. But when justice is denied its public status and becomes private, almost by definition it turns into injustice. Something similar has happened to beauty. Fascism accelerated the disappearance of public beauty by repressing or manipulating the *piazza*.

The fascist speed-up in displacing beauty only heightened a general Western trend. Through the Renaissance, a major portion of every city was devoted to collective functions and had to correspond to collective aesthetic criteria. When growing numbers of the wealthy built palaces for their private enjoyment of beauty, the facades of these structures nonetheless still addressed the public eye and were meant to satisfy it. But in the modern era beauty has gradually withdrawn from the public square, concentrating itself in a shrinking fashion into collective transport—the great liners—then the automobile, and thence into domestic appliances, individual style and fashion, and finally, beneath clothing onto the skin itself with tattooing and piercing.

A moment's historical reflection reminds us that in the West real beauty originally had almost nothing to do with clothing. The Greeks, who had a much stronger aesthetic sense than the Romans, wore very simple clothing, and very little of it. The Renaissance way of dressing could be aesthetic but also excessively extravagant. At any rate, it tended to follow the drive toward individual creation and expression. Descending to modern fashion, we arrive at neither beauty nor individual expression but essentially the badge or brand, the commercial logo. A given fashion declares its worth through labeling, the presence of a standardized name. I still remember how, in the 1950s and 60s, many Italian young people would cut the labels from their clothes— which were then beginning to sport these insignia *on the outside.* Nowadays, what makes a garment worthwhile in the fashion game is the label—not what is unique, but what it has in common with many others. Thus, the act of dressing has become part of an anti-individuation process, the attempt to buy rather than build a personality: an unconscious effort immediately to possess what should be the result of gradual self-assessment and personal development.

Fashion often has more to say about psychological problems than it does about beauty. A man at home alone who dresses in Armani has difficulties accepting himself as he is. A party at which everybody dresses in Armani is the clothed manifesto of a generation that has given up on individuation.

Of all the masters of drama, Aeschylus best knew what aesthetics are in their constant interplay with ethos and justice. Twenty-five centuries ago he denounced those who avoid taking the risk of achieving actualization while remaining in the public realm. "Many prefer to appear rather than to be, thus committing injustice," he said.[3] For the Greeks, what went wrong was the implicit arrogance of wanting to catch the eye rather than striving for beauty, which was—and still is—defined by the consensus of the social eye. Greek beauty was sought after in the creation of something observed by and belonging to many, most notably a temple or statue. Beauty as something owned privately is a rather modern perception.

The survival of beauty under modern conditions has hardly anything to do with the Italian past, but perhaps everything to do with an American future. On the one hand, most American mass culture has visibly repressed the aesthetic polarity. But on the other hand, however much or little of beauty is being perceived and enjoyed around the world, it is nowadays headed toward some *palazzo* in the United States. Sensitivity to the necessity of sharing beauty—for in a certain sense beauty is real only if it is put into circulation—was born in Europe, but now grows in American museums and foundations. One of the most challenging future tasks of our dull and obese Western world is the re-aestheticizing of its values, through the re-opening of its *palazzi* to the *piazza*. That re-opening of the gateway of balance between aesthetics and justice, beauty and ethics, is the paradoxical endeavor of mass culture, and therefore a predominantly American task: a task that, because of cultural, historical, and economic conditions, remains an almost exclusively American possibility.[4]

CHAPTER 6

Ethics Again

Having expressed discomfort with the prospect of ethics separated from its original union with aesthetics, let us go back to ethics proper.

Analysis is a sort of humanistic knowledge. It is by no means a true science, a natural science. This implies that analysis cannot be morally neutral like chemistry, which can be used to develop either healing remedies or poison gas. Humanistic or social sciences (*Geistwissenschaften*, in Dilthey's term adopted by much of European philosophy) take their stand, or establish their basis, on the human being and human society. Indeed, following an Italian and French tradition, what I am calling humanistic or social sciences have been called in English *moral sciences* since the nineteenth century.[1]

The core aim of analysis is ethical: analysis aims at doing battle with lies—first and foremost, of course, the lies that we tell ourselves. We do not struggle for years with dreams and unconscious fantasies because it is entertaining. We do it because we strive for more sincerity. We want to understand. Life is too precious for us to spend it only among conventions and lies (which are so often frighteningly interwoven).

There is a corollary to this aim. If analysis is about transparency and respect, then it cannot thrive in a society that avoids these qualities. This is easily proved. In fascist Italy, analysis was not forbidden, yet it remained almost nonexistent. Not by chance, the few analysts and their tiny band of patients were almost always opponents of the regime. Nonetheless, in those years the few proponents of analysis claimed that it was a neutral technique, not a moral endeavor. Had analysis managed somehow to grow during the fascist era, the task of enforcing upon it an ethical code would have been more difficult than nowadays, for the uncritical use of power and male chauvinism were deeply embedded in society. How can a specific social science avoid carrying the traits of the milieu in which it is born? Yet even nowadays this historical conditioning has rendered it more difficult to introduce ethical standards later, long after analysis had already developed into a relevant social reality.

Our aim is to examine the ethics of therapy as one branch of general ethics. Branches do not exist alone, floating in the air. We should never lose sight of the whole tree, and, if we care for a tree, common sense tells us to start with the roots.

Today under the heading "the ethics of psychotherapy" one finds many books, whose covers commonly point to the whole tree of ethics. However, the pages inside concern themselves almost exclusively with the branches, or various sets of rules. The least amount of concern is devoted to the roots, those values out of which the plant grows. This ratio of priorities resembles the absurd intentions of a man who enters a temple to pray without asking which God is worshipped there.

These texts offer to help translate a value system into daily professional reality, but they do not describe their root values, and possibly are not even aware of them. True, roots are usually invisible, under the earth's surface. But Freud and Jung's ideas correspond precisely to discovering the importance of what is not directly perceived. The fact that the roots are not exposed becomes, far from an excuse for not looking further, an obligation for the analytical psychologist to look closely indeed.

CHAPTER 7

The Gray Zone

Because psychological analysis more often bases itself on images and metaphors than on precise concepts, at this point we will borrow an image from a writer.

Primo Levi, an Italian Jew and an industrial chemist in private life, became an internationally known writer with a book describing his experience of survival in Auschwitz.[1] In later essays, Primo Levi elaborated his theme from an ethical perspective, specifically identifying what he called the "gray zone."[2] Fiction and movies have frequently exploited the suffering of Auschwitz prisoners for commercial purposes. In these black-and-white representations, the arduous task of ethical elaboration is usually avoided. Good and evil are predefined and simplified: they are not the real text, but only a pre-text, whose radical separation into moral opposites is conducive to that voyeurism that seeks out displays of sadism. During those same years, Levi also wrote powerful pieces in the Italian press against this ethical distortion by both print and film media. Because his analysis of Auschwitz derives from his personal attempt to give individual evaluations of those he had met there, it constantly comes up against ethical complexities.

In the extermination camps, besides black-and-white realities there was open ground for a vast "gray zone." While immorality was ever present, it was regularly intermingled with humanity to such an extent that it became impossible to establish clear lines of distinction.

The basis for this gray zone was the root value of survival: life as such always has a higher value than most of our rules. Daily food allowances were part of the extermination project, in that they were insufficient for survival. Under such circumstances, stealing, cheating, and other practices that are normally unacceptable become necessary. On the side of the captors, favoritism, breaches of rules, corruption, and the tolerance of misbehavior can become virtues among guards and supervising technicians. (Levi survived because, as a chemist, he was assigned to a laboratory—a circumstance that at least theoretically implicated him in Nazi military production.) In such conditions, a handbook reliance on the simplified polarities of good and evil contributes to neither a moral education nor a debate on ethics, whereas an analysis of the gray zone nourishes both.[3]

In a word, a principled examination of pure good and evil offers little or nothing to an ethical understanding of societies in an extreme, transitional phase. The gray zone supplies better navigation. And not only that: in order to overcome horror and destruction, and to further the process of extreme transition in a favorable way, often the best choice is to *intentionally create* a gray zone.

Let us think of the many unjust regimes that have been overthrown by sudden violent revolutions: enantiadromic transposition supplants revolution, for after a while the good has become evil, and the evil good. Spain's colonies in the Americas rebelled against the imperial yoke, but many of them turned into corrupt or dictatorial states. Tyrannical czarist Russia, after the hopes of the revolution were betrayed, soon became the tyrannical Soviet Union. And so on. Over time in a collective ethos, nothing viewed through the lens of absolute good and evil seems to deeply change.[4]

It requires a certain ethical clarity and courage to stand clear of the ethically absolutizing perspective. For a courageous application of such psychological wisdom on a collective scale we must turn to South Africa and its Truth and Reconciliation Commission. Standing before it, both the triumphant African Nationalists and the losing white supremacists had to confess their crimes. Through a full and spontaneous confession, all those who viewed themselves as heroic fighters had to show their dirty hands in public. Only through a thorough and uncoerced confession could a person be granted amnesty and readmitted into civil life. The civic dough of the new South African society was kneaded together with the earth and mud of the gray zone.

The radical courage of the Commission consisted in aiming not at purity, but at ethical complexity and its elaboration.[5] Caveat lector, therefore: official history, which aims at purity, is very often official stupidity and immorality. Its absolutizing value categories are notoriously fluid in their application: if the rebels win, those killers are promoted to the status of heroic patriots, whereas if they lose, they are damned as simple terrorists. In Italian schoolbooks one finds Pietro Micca, a predecessor of today's suicide bombers, extolled for a desperate expedient that he carried out more than two centuries ago. He probably attained this status because of the traditional Italian lack of discipline, but also because of a certain reluctance, not at all despicable, to be well equipped with weapons of mass destruction. Micca was placed in charge of a large reserve cache of explosives the enemy was about to capture. As he couldn't find a proper fuse with which to safely detonate the ammo dump from a safe distance, he decided to wait until he was nearly overwhelmed and then ignite it all the same, ending up blown to pieces together with everyone else.

CHAPTER 8

Narration

The psyche is the habitat of complexity (another denomination of Jung's psychology is "Complex Psychology"—in fact the original one designated by him) and of ambivalence. And it is so not occasionally, but structurally. In previous writings, I have tried to link the birth of analysis not with a given stage in the evolution of psychiatry or psychology, but instead with a crucial early stage in the development of Western narrative.[1]

While psychotherapy is a recent, limited Western discipline, narration has been essential in every age and civilization. The framing of meaning through the making of story is essential to the healing of both the collective and individual souls. The backbone of Western narration (and possibly of all narration) is tragedy, which is essentially the tale of the intertwined helplessness of the human condition and the ambivalence of the human being. Only in the twentieth century has tragic narration gradually been supplanted by a new narrative form, the anti-tragic Hollywood story. Yet even with such a widespread trend before us, there is no gainsaying the fact that the recounting of our complexity and our ambivalence is an eternal, natural necessity that cannot simply be eliminated. Therefore we would expect to find the collective disappearance of tragic narration compensated by its resurgence elsewhere. And indeed, it has taken a new, private and individual form, in keeping with bourgeois culture's focus on private life and individualism. This new form is no longer a collective ritual like drama, but a private ritual, namely analysis. And analysis, we must remind ourselves, has emerged not because of the need to fight neuroses—which is hardly a novel battle, and which had already taken different forms—but because of the ancient necessity to fashion a container for our ambivalence that can render it meaningful through narration.

If we now translate all these reflections on our complexity into ethical terms, we might well conclude that *ambivalence is an essential gray zone of the soul*. Just as complexity tends to disappear from collective narration in modern and contemporary culture, and must seek out an internalized refuge for its acknowledgment elsewhere, so too does the moral issue in its fullness depart from mainstream collective accounts to seek out a safe and strong enough individual ritual container for its whole meaning.

Here too rests the ethical approach of Erich Neumann: the real fight between good and evil cannot be solved on the battlefield, but takes the form of an elaboration of the inner relationship with our dark side (the Jungian archetype of the shadow). Since depth psychology has not only officially but also actually become part of our knowledge, we cannot confine our responsibility to what we consciously know and collectively acknowledge. We are compelled to admit that we must account for the problematic aspects of our personality, which we cannot perceive directly but which nonetheless can be rendered more conscious through constant elaboration and critical self-analysis.

The sentimental heroes of the commercial fable factory do not tell real tales. They simply entertain us, and we forget them once the spell of simplifying, briefly thrilling or intriguing narration is over. They are essentially flat, and hence cannot project a shadow. They produce detachment instead of real identification. They tranquilize us—in fact, they an-aesthetize us, and not by chance, for they erase our aesthetic perceptions.[2] The formulae of mass culture drive us back upon an old Greek argument: only the tragic hero triggers identification, by inspiring pity and terror.[3]

Which is also to say that a genuine hero is tragic beyond conventional notions of goodness—that such a hero is complex, and can only dwell in the gray zone. The historical figure of Brutus, in Shakespeare's handling, in spite of loving Caesar chooses to kill him, his own adoptive father, fearing that Caesar is drifting irreversibly toward tyranny. Shakespeare does not depict him as a traditional hero who out of goodness gives battle to evil. Instead, he sets forth Brutus's conflicting motives, plays out the action through all of them, enlists the audience in that full interplay, and draws all together in the gray zone. Brutus's heroic struggle takes place not on the battlefield of civics, tyrannicide, and republican virtue, but in the complexity of his soul.

CHAPTER 9

Growing Unethical?

Unethical behavior is on the rise in many professions. On the one hand, this is indisputably the consequence of a gradual erosion of traditional social values in every corner of the world. On the other hand, it is also the result of technological progress and the unopposed sweep of global capitalistic forces, both of which provide new occasions for crime.

Sitting in front of your computer, you are inches from a tool that makes theft in many respects easier and "cleaner" than robbing a bank. There is no risk of being shot, or of seeing blood. In the isolation and anonymity of your room, you do not sense the violent social rupture that is unavoidable in any robbery. What you steal is immaterial, is stored virtually, and is transferred with the speed of a magician's hand. All this helps you to perceive the operation as an unreal game, one more function of your play-station. Instinctive inhibition gets lost.

Similarly, in modern warfare, the number of victims has skyrocketed, not only because of advances in destructive technology but also because of a corresponding repression of natural inhibitions. Slicing through the body of an enemy with a cutlass exposes you to disgust and to the contamination of his suffering. By pressing one button that launches a sequence of missiles or bombs, however, you can kill a whole mass of people with no corresponding exposure to the facts.[1]

Likewise, the newfangled economic criminality, being mostly an individual, anonymous, and virtual activity, has proliferated and prospered. In its realm the psyche becomes flat and shadowless, like the computer screen. This sort of crime does not produce guilt feelings. The ethical task described by Neumann thereby becomes increasingly difficult to acknowledge, let alone confront.

The American author Jeremy Rifkin has poignantly explained how the expression "free market" may soon mean nothing at all—not because freedom is vanishing, but because the market is.[2] The market was a place of open access and free movement (the *piazza* or public square) where people could meet and freely exchange their goods. This open space of the commons, this *res publicum,* or "civic thing," has been gradually replaced by other realities, further and further away (the stock exchange retains a floor and a gavel but operates by remote buying and selling), or less and less material (the Internet). The market tends in the end toward virtual reality, to which only certain people under certain circumstances have access. The dispersal-based importance of access has supplanted the central position of the market.

Rifkin, however, has described only the economic consequences of market disappearance or dispersal. We are left wondering about the huge psychological ones. The disappearance of the market would correspond to the vanishing of the *piazza,* which has been supplanted by a virtual *palazzo,* an invisible kingdom of access. This de-realization or anonymization, in turn, corresponds to the entire dispersal of a face-to-face community, of its culture and collective psychology. The contract was originally a handshake—*contractus* from *contrahere* means drawn together, not dispersed—and in that intimate physical act the potential for shame and collective reprobation was—the statistics of economical crime are telling us—more powerful than the fear of lawyers and the courts.

When the community disappears, morals are inevitably diminished, because morals are the standards enforced by the pressure of the community itself, notably symbolized in a handshake's pressure. Social control makes anyone more aware of one's shadow.

Neumann has suggested that, as long as we are not overwhelmed by a new complexity, we should be content with the clear lines and generalizing criteria of the "old ethics." The explosion of new technologies and new economic conditions, however, is depriving us of access to the communal basis for that older clarity, forcing us onto new, uncharted ethical ground: an immense gray zone whose grayness is hermetic, for it has less to do with moral complexity and more to do with invisibility and unaccountability.

Psychotherapy in the depth dimension is at home with such factors, itself being hospitable to the hermetic function. Analysis, fortunately, is no beneficiary of technological progress. From our perspective, this fact carries with it the advantage that the *piazza* of the psyche does not disappear.

New techno-wizardries and a newly rough global economy have not offered to psychotherapists novel possibilities for unethical behavior. Bucking the trend toward increasingly unethical activity, it is likely that in recent decades ethical transgressions in analysis and psychotherapy have not grown. On a per capita basis, they even should have decreased. But neither is psychotherapy a neutral quantity. It is a living plant, sensitive to the culture in which its roots are planted. Whatever pollutes this soil can damage psychotherapy as well.

CHAPTER 10

The Ethics of Analysis

A circular linkage joins ethics with therapy and analysis, which can be the objects of ethics. However, they can also rapidly become active subjects. This fact leads us to examine, along with ethics in the practice of analysis, the ethics *of* analysis itself.

We live in a world of increasing tragic loneliness and decreasing attention to social connections, the anomie that is a common root for both growing pathology in the psyche and growing crime in society. In this respect, analysis itself dwells in the gray zone, for on the one hand it has a tremendous power for restoring sound human relations, but on the other has often been criticized as the final contributor to an irremediable excess of individualism and narcissism. In a world in which social values still claimed superiority to individual ones, paying a highly skilled professional over many years simply to listen to your inner difficulties would have been immoral—or simply unthinkable.

Today, however, an ethical value inheres in the very conditions of analytic work. Running against the contemporary deterioration of humanistic values, in analysis time is still time. There is no hurry; time does not get compressed. And speech is still speech. Analysis is the zone of liberty for discourse, there being no taboos against expression, and there likewise being not only the possibility for sincerity but even the obligation to practice it. Meanwhile, the shadow cast by these values insists on laying out its gray expanse: is not the fact that one agrees to pay for years of an artificial and asymmetric relationship a conclusive admission that one belongs to some sort of postmodern species of humanity, incapable of natural relationships?

The gray zone turns out, however, to include the healing factor. The capacity to restore human relations through the analytical process is conditioned by the quality of an ancient procedure of wound dressing and the votive acknowledgment of renewed health, which today we technically call transference and countertransference. Without a relationship, analysis and therapy risk becoming intellectual processes that barely touch our emotions.

And here one should ask the timely question: how has the intensity of transference and countertransference actually evolved over the course of the last few decades? It is not unreasonable to hypothesize that such intensity has decreased, for many factors converge in suggesting this development. First of all, the average frequency of sessions has decreased, and with it the emotional tone of the link between therapist and patient. Secondly, the (in itself necessary) increase—and increased definition—of boundaries, and the publicity of analytical abuses, have rendered the attitudes of both parties in analysis more defensive. Thirdly, the increased awareness of gender issues, and the frequent abuses of female patients by male analysts in the first several generations of practice, has influenced female patients nowadays mostly to seek out women analysts (who were scarce in the founding generation) and male patients male analysts. In this way, the most "risky" kind of relationship—the one most likely to occasion an erotic transference—is in principle avoided. But the whole attitude might correspond to avoiding the risk of intense relationships altogether (in keeping with our tendency toward a "society of insurance"). If so, then our obsession with safety has taken another toll. The trend, at any rate, corresponds to an avoidance of real encounters with the other. Instead of confrontation with alterity, the exclusion of it prevails. There is every reason to doubt, however, that such self-protective estrangement from the "external other" is the best start for a confrontation with "the other inside us."

Finally and fourthly in this catalog of conditions for decreasing intensity in the analytic relationship, the question arises: because psychotherapy cannot avoid sharing the values of the society it stems from, to what extent has analysis lately been bent toward individualistic fulfillment and away from making relationship a top priority? If this question has merit, then the attention now paid to boundaries in psychotherapy might be seen as a particular case of the overall devaluation of relationships: instead of working against that tendency, analysis may have unconsciously inserted itself into the trend. If that is indeed the case, then instead of becoming a positive new acquisition, boundaries could reassume their ancient negative undertone of separation.

I would like us to reflect upon this possibility. Viewed from within, as an internal affair and an individual responsibility, boundaries acquire psychological substance and maximum value when they are seen as if they were moveable or perhaps permeable—that is, capable of opening up zones defined wholly by neither one nor another moral quality. Once again, I would suggest that we fulfill our ethical duties by placing ourselves not on the "right" side, but in the mixed and intermediate gray zone; that we strive not for an ethics of purity, but for the ethically problematic. Like the most desirable parent suggested by Donald Winnicott, such an ethical attitude could prove to be only "good-enough ethics," but *only,* this time, in the nonexclusive, nonoppositional sense that permits us to include our own shadow in the reckoning.

Part Two

ANALYSIS:

ETHICAL PERSPECTIVES

ON PSYCHOTHERAPY

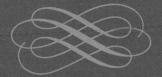

CHAPTER 11

Processing

Before focusing specifically on psychotherapeutic ethics, we have addressed ethical values in general. This background is necessary because humanistic disciplines cannot be neutral. Not only do they have ethical premises or values, but also—unlike the natural sciences—their practice implies a continuity of ethical positions.

This implication confronts all of us with an uncomfortable demand. Exhausted by the complexities of personal psychology and collective history, we long for what seems to be the clarity of the natural sciences. Yet the scientist too is only on a short vacation from history, the briefest furlough from ethical nonneutrality. The scientist too is tormented by the complexity of human guilt as soon as he has to deal with persons behind his version of the paradise screen, the veil of natural law. Let us now turn to examine the relationship between laws in the natural sciences and the moral law that operates in humanistic disciplines.

Back in Italy after he had survived the concentration camps, Primo Levi resumed his work as a chemist. Employed in the production of paint, he had to correspond with a German factory from which his firm imported several chemical components. In 1967, Levi had to lodge a complaint about a large shipment of resin that failed to solidify properly. The affair could have caused a significant economic loss. On both sides, the correspondence carefully balanced commercial politeness with the possibility that damages might be sought in the courts. Levi's German counterpart was obsessively exact, stipulating which hidden causes could be investigated and which chemical laws and procedures could be attempted before the Italian company could return the shipment as useless.

From a series of the smallest details in this exchange, which he quickly verified, Levi found out that the Dr. Müller with whom he was corresponding had been his supervisor at the chemical factory at Buna, which had been attached to Auschwitz. Levi's survival was due in large part to the fact that, being a chemist, he had been assigned to the Buna plant where synthetic rubber was made, a critical feature of the German war economy.

Müller had in fact been one of those prototypical gray men who populate the ethical gray zone. Incapable of criticizing the rules he was carrying out, he was also incapable of ignoring the suffering of the camp victims and enduring his corresponding guilt feelings. As a result, he was excessively polite, attempted to provide material help to his conscript workers, and took refuge in the obsessive execution of his work.

Having identified Dr. Müller, Dr. Levi began a second, private correspondence that ran parallel to the official commercial one. In it he was looking for other causes and other laws, laws that are nonscientific and inexact—*ex-actus* indicates a derivation from material action rather than moral effort—but which firmly correspond to human values and constantly imply ethical responsibilities. These questions obsessed Levi's life—and they probably played a role in his death (Levi committed suicide in 1987). How could an apparently innocent, absolutely normal and noncriminal person such as Müller have become—however minimally and benevolently—a part of the Nazi extermination project?

These questions frame a debate that belongs to psychology and to the humanistic sciences. Unlike a debate about laws and processes in chemistry, each part of this inquiry into human action allows for different points of view and easily overflows the confines of its specific discipline: human ethical behaviors equally concern psychology, anthropology, sociology, and the other humanistic sciences.

As Levi describes events in the "Vanadium" chapter of his *Periodic*

Table (1975), during his first correspondence with Müller he managed to ascertain the necessary answers to the chemical questions. In his second, personal exchange of letters, however, he drifted unsystematically toward intimacy. Müller showed limits in his psychological understanding. He was trying, with little success, to forgive both himself and his superiors. He wrote to Levi declaring that he intended to travel to Italy, asking Levi for a meeting in person. At the prospect of this encounter Levi experienced unspeakable and contradictory storms of emotion, which as it turned out would remain without resolution. Instead of Müller himself came a letter from his wife, announcing his utterly unexpected, premature death.

We expect the values of a specific branch of human knowledge to be compatible with the general values of the whole tree—that each branch of knowledge will accord ethically with the human society in which its applications operate.

In the case of psychoanalysis, the relationship between branch and tree is particularly clear. As I have stressed in my other writings, the main contribution of psychoanalysis to the twentieth century is not one of individual therapy. At the end of the century, humanity's self-image was very different from the one at its beginning, owing to dramatic cultural influences. Besides two world wars, the communist revolution, the technological and atomic revolutions, economic globalization, and so on, psychoanalysis has played its own decisive role. In contrast to certain of these influential factors, it has brought about a bloodless revolution, and uniquely among them it began originally as something specialized, an individual therapy, but ended as a therapy of the whole culture. An "age of introspection" has been set in motion by it, affecting every aspect of art and literature.

Therefore a deep link between general values and the specific values of psychoanalysis has become both a necessary condition and a goal of professional ethics. In the same way, any review of psychoanalysis and analytical psychology from this perspective should prove that their "constitutional principles" do not contradict those of the society that plays host to them.

According to Jung, the highest value of analytical psychology—and of depth psychology in general—consists in the deepening of consciousness.[1] The link between this specialized ethical task and the general, factual morality of society stands evident. Understanding ourselves better, becoming more aware of our complex motivations and of our complexes, we can try to ease our inner contradictions. We can attempt to ameliorate destructive tensions within ourselves before attempting to "ameliorate" conflicts in the outer world by destroying others whom we consider evil. Had Hitler and Stalin worked toward more awareness of their own shadows before projecting them with fury onto national groups or social classes, the twentieth century would not have turned into the bloodiest beast of history.[2] Of course, their failures to do so were taken up by millions of others as well. The analysis of psychic processes that aims at deepening consciousness is not only a matter of specialized techniques for certain individuals, it is also an ethical endeavor that concerns everybody without exception.

How does this ethical ideal translate into practice from a Jungian perspective?

The Western mind is split in a particular way, both from the unconscious parts of the psyche and from a natural understanding of psychic phenomena. Scientific progress has generated a mental functioning that automatically tends toward generalizations. Scientific knowledge tries to determine uniform laws. Yet, as Jung observed in 1957, in *The Undiscovered Self,* "the more a theory lays claim to universal validity, the less capable it is of doing justice to the individual facts. . . . Any theory formulates an ideal average." On the contrary, "the distinctive quality about real facts . . . is their individuality. . . . One could say that the real picture consists of nothing but exceptions to the rule." In conclusion, then: "If I want to understand an individual human being, I must lay aside all scientific knowledge of the average man and discard all theories in order to adopt a completely new and unprejudiced attitude. I can only approach the task of understanding [*Verständnis*] with a free and open mind, whereas knowledge [*Erkenntniss*] of man, or insight into human character, presupposes all sorts of knowledge about mankind in general."[3]

Let us sum up matters thus far. What is ethical for analytical psychology is first and foremost the process of reaching deeper consciousness. This process differs in its essential aims from those of scientific knowledge, with its tendency to produce general laws. Jung aimed at the understanding of the individual, unrepeatable single mind. The objects he had in mind were uniqueness as opposed to uniformity, justice as opposed to law, and understanding as opposed to knowing.

Knowledge of psychological causes is not generalizable in the way that the knowledge of scientific causes is. Simple scientific knowledge, apart from the uses made of it, can be considered ethically neutral. Knowledge in itself is in play, and not necessarily the human person. But somewhere down the road, a human being will use this knowledge as a tool, and that action will imply a responsibility. At that point, the dynamics will take place on a sociological, philosophical, anthropological, or psychological ground: the common ground of the humanistic sciences, which implies an ethical stance. Scientific knowledge alone does not respond to Kant's practical imperative, whereas humanistic knowledge does.

If, as we have argued since the beginning, the psyche in its totality is the foundational structural residence of ambivalence and complexity, then analytical psychology must accept the fact that it is a container of ambivalence and complexity even when ruling on ethical issues. The act of making rulings indeed becomes an almost impossible task. Yet, the professionals of psychotherapy who are in charge of ethical issues must reach conclusions. And these conclusions must be clear and communicable to the public at large.

The most typical task of an ethics committee belonging to a psychoanalytic association is the processing of complaints. Normally, the committee will be composed of analysts—having analytical values—who are entrusted with the task of ensuring that, in their concrete application, these values do not contradict those of society, while at the same time rendering individual justice as best as they can in the given case.

The most frequent kind of complaint concerns abuses of transference. Because the relationship between patient and analyst pursues analytical values—the deepening of awareness—it can become more intimate than any other human relationship. It is this quality of intimacy, more or less, that we call transference. Transference can be abused by transforming it into a sexual relationship—or also in other ways, for instance transforming it into an economic, religious, or ideological partnership. What is unethical is not the presence of any one of these elements *in itself.* Sexuality is often indirectly present in the form of an erotically tinged transference or of erotic narratives from the patient; economics enters into the contractual payments; and both ideology and religion arise in the frequent need to share the same ideas and beliefs in the analytical relationship. No limited, conscious, and declared amount of eros, economy, ideology, or religion is unethical in analysis. What becomes unethical is the transformation of the intensity in the transference from its service as a means of deeper consciousness into an instrument of egoistic gratification for the analyst. An ab-use is a use that has gone astray, and therefore contradicts Kant's practical imperative of retaining the patient as a final end. In its most common form, such abuse uses the dependency of the patient to entice him or her into a sexual relationship with the analyst, or into a financial investment with the analyst, or to convert the patient to the ideology, the religion, the sect, or whatever persuasion to which the analyst adheres and believes in.

But we can also apply Kant from a more psychological perspective, in the way of Neumann's "new ethics." In this view, the analyst also submits to abuse within. That is, his shadow misuses his ego. From this perspective, evil does not correspond to an evil intention, but to a lack of consciousness: to the fact that an unconscious drive is guiding the ego, of which the analyst remains unaware. To be sure, in normal life it is a common occurrence for the conscious ego to be influenced by unconscious shadow-drives. But the life of the analyst proves to be no exception.

In a groundbreaking text, Jonathan Glover analyzed recent history from an ethical perspective.[4] He identifies "human resources" as the main psychological defenses against drifts toward the immoral behavior that is typical of extreme political situations.[5] Natural tendencies to feel respect and sympathy are the most important of these human resources.

Sympathy is a Greek word meaning to suffer together, to identify with (*syn-*). To the paradoxical and tragic nature of analysis belongs a structural form of sympathy on the part of the professional, which responds to the transference and is called countertransference. When it crosses over a certain edge, this sympathy dispenses with the necessary ethical balance in that paradoxical situation. The tragic element in ethical equilibrium necessarily observes limits. And so a self-propelled countertransference, because it can become a goal in itself, severs its moorings in the world like a boat whose journey has no destination.

The capacity for identification is a fundamental human response. But, as both "new ethics" and old proverbs remind us, the devil can hide precisely in the best of human qualities. Of course, it is not through sympathy in itself that a therapy can damage the patient. Rather it is the excessive—and often unconsciously egoistic—expression of sympathy that distracts from the real goal of the therapy—the healing of the patient—while increasing the patient's dependency on the therapist. In its turn, the expression of sympathy can be driven on both sides by unconscious motives: by the analyst's desire to seduce the patient and by the patient's desire to promote approval, care, and love on the part of the therapist, instead of promoting one's own independence and growth.

Let us revert to our example of the Ethics Committee in a psychotherapeutic association, whose task it is to investigate abuses of transference.

We have verified the fact that the constituent values of analytical work—to pursue more truth through inner search—are consistent with the general constituent values of the society as a whole, because for society, too, truth is one of the highest values. The committee must ascertain whether the analyst has deviated from his or her task, the psychological search. This abuse of professional function would breach specific professional rules, but also be in collision with society's basic rules. By doing all it can to process the case, the Ethics Committee abides by both the "constitution" of analytical activity and the general "constitution" of the whole society, where exploitation coinciding with inequality of position (adult versus child, officer holding institutional power versus common citizen, and so forth) should be prevented.

If the allegations fit this pattern, the processing takes place.

The approach to each and every verdict is so delicate a matter that the best way to proceed seems, from every point of view, to collect as much information as possible. Yet this way of going about things can have massive drawbacks precisely from a psychological point of view. Every court case that takes too long ends up displeasing everybody. There is an old aphorism in Ethics Committees that says that when the processing goes on too long, in the end both the plaintiff and the defendant will be upset. English usage refers both to courtroom drama and *the judicial process,* but the Italian language reflects such wisdom even more plainly in its adaptation of the Latin root: a trial is a *processo.* A good piece of processing runs like a well-paced trial.

Analysis, as we have said, is the homeland of ambivalence. Naturally, then, the institutions called to exercise a judicial function over it must also face and deal with ambivalence.

Let me remind us all that the work of an Ethics Committee, although carried out by analysts, relies essentially on facts, not on interpretations. The committee's members try to understand and take into account unconscious motivations, but these cannot center their rulings. Members are commissioned to act outside our specialized analytical container and therefore can be satisfied with their results if these manage, by way of our embracing analogy, to apply the general rules of society.

Likewise, the other participants in the process operate on an equally "secular"—factual, legalistic, and nonpsychological—ground. But unlike the committee, they have a manifest and clear interest in doing so. From a psychological point of view, we notice that at this point the assignment of responsibility commands the procedure, so that projection and not the inner search becomes almost automatically the leading criterion for functioning.

The defendant must provide a defense. The plaintiff or complainant must provide new evidence, if it is available. Which implies a new defense. At the end of the procedure, once the committee has ruled, both sides must have the right to appeal. As this sequence unfolds, following the analogy with a court case, the parties look desperately for more responsibilities to be found in—or projected onto—their counterparts. In doing so, they do not simply remain *passive* in their analytic capacities: they sooner or later *actively suppress* them. The processing compels them, as energetically as possible, to erase the awareness of their own shadow.

If we look at this from the perspective of psychopathology, we notice that while paranoid attitudes have been an illness fought by analysis, they have become useful allies in the adversarial ethical procedure. If we look at the same matter from Neumann's perspective, we can observe that the old psychology of the scapegoat returns in triumph. The "old ethics" takes its revenge on the vulnerable new one, so recent and fragile and achieved with such great effort. This outcome is particularly sad, because ethical complaints derive essentially from shadow aspects, which have grown stronger than the ego. We would do well to inscribe a sort of Neumann's "ethical imperative," parallel to Kant's, among the inspiring criteria of the therapeutic ethics code, in the form of exhortations to be responsible not only for what one consciously knows but also for those shadow aspects of which one could become more aware. However, such a wise reminder of the ethics already at work *in* analysis gets practically eliminated precisely by the procedural survey of ethics *and* analysis—by the processing responsible for surveying the implementation of correct professional, and hence, psychological, values.

In order that a verdict may be reached, every procedure requires agreement on a basic reconstruction of the facts. But the role of the shadow, and of other unconscious elements, can be construed only through interpretation, which will be denied by the party that has any interest in doing so. The "new ethics" is therefore expunged from the findings by the lack of consent to its place in ethical processing.

From the strict perspective of our analytic values, such processing undoes hard-won analytical attitudes by the effort to reinstate projection at the expense of self-criticism (hetero-analysis replacing self-analysis)—in short, a *counter-analysis* is set in motion by the official procedure, which can go on for a number of years.

In my opinion, this undoing of the ethics *in* analysis explains why such deep feelings of frustration, sadness, and futility are often experienced by both parties at the end of the procedure. This fact better accounts for the outcome than does the humanly unsatisfying ruling into which such deep feelings are projected. A ruling is always human and imperfect, and one that comes after a long procedure leaves particular frustration, because in the meanwhile further bitterness has accumulated. But what renders the procedure of an analytical Ethics Committee structurally frustrating is something else. Both parties involved in such a procedure evidently believe in analytical values and in Neumann's new ethics, otherwise one would not have become an analyst and the other would not have entered analysis. But in order to carry on with the consensual arbitration they are compelled, to a very large extent, to betray their shared belief.

*A*t this point, let us consider a particular case.

The unethical event in itself is quite clear. A sexual abuse of transference had taken place. The act occurred quite a few years before the analysand speaks out—but because it fell within the statutes of limitation, and in keeping with the fact that the re-elaboration of similar events can long remain latent and in any case was very painful and drawn out, a complaint was lodged. The abuse was clear and the analyst was sanctioned accordingly. Yet, an already lengthy suffering was prolonged by sidetrackings, appeals, and the emergence of collateral abuses and lateral intromissions.

Let us unfold the details of the sequence. As often happens in similar circumstances, the patient had tried to restart analysis soon after the event. But, due to both material and psychological difficulties, this was possible only after some time had passed. The development of this new analysis was painful but positive; the entire story of the abuse would surface, and subsequent review of the second analysis leads one to believe that during its course both cathartic and introspective goals were attained.

After the end of this second analysis, without any detectable interruption, patient and analyst remained in contact for a number of years. It was during this phase that the patient submitted an official complaint. And it was the second analyst who became, in agreement with the official plaintiff, the second protagonist. This alter-ego wrote to the Ethics Committee in an official capacity many times, stating among other things that he/she knew everything not only about the abuse but also about the genesis of the complaint. One letter specified that even during the years after the analysis had ended, and on a regular basis, the analyst kept encouraging the patient to take up the fight and gave advice. Only gradually did it emerge that the assistance given to the patient was part of a more complex ideological activity on the part of the analyst. For, shortly after the finding was given, that analyst tried to set in motion a reform of the ethical procedures for the analytical association.

The first analyst had blatantly transgressed Kant's practical imperative by turning the patient from an end in herself into an instrument. But the second analyst too seemed intent on acting contrary to Kant's ethical categories. Instead of treating the patient as a transcendent end, the second analyst subtly abused the patient by making the person into an instrument of the analyst's political agenda.

From the viewpoint of psychopathology, the case confirmed the observation that abused persons tend to put themselves in positions where they are abused again. From being abused sexually by the first analyst, the patient had fallen, with the second analysis, into a situation of potential ideological abuse.

From the viewpoint of professional analytical associations and their codes of ethics, however, the case confirmed that to a large extent we remain constantly immersed, as small collectives of colleagues, in a gray zone. There had been undeniable progress in the work accomplished by the second analysis, yet both the new analyst and the patient had remained unaware of essential elements of their own shadows. The processing of the complaint did not extricate them from this condition. Ideally, what might have helped would have been the application of Neumann's approach—the basic revision of ethics from the point of view of analytical psychology. That would have allowed the Ethics Committee, in processing the complaint against the first analyst, to clarify the persistence of problematic attitudes in the second analysis as well. But that proved to be impossible. The committee was tasked with reviewing a complaint concerning only the first analyst, and had to face the fact that ethical principles often can be enforced only upon the past situation and not upon its current and ongoing consequences.

Analysis is a typically human situation. Abstract knowledge about analysis does not help much unless it is coupled with personal experience and suffering. Because of this paramount fact, all the main analytical schools insist that the most important part of training a new analyst must be a personal analysis.

*L*et us go back to our initial question. Can the constituent values of our work remain consistent with those of society at large, upon which the search for responsibilities and the application of sanctions carried out by an Ethics Committee are based?

After reviewing the typical facts about processing in these situations, we cannot avoid the feeling that there is a threshold beyond which what constitutes these general operational principles for modern society leaves our analytic values *destitute*. In other terms, the psychotherapeutic endeavor, when drawn into adversarial processing, can turn what Jonathan Glover calls "human resources" from values into dangers. In the regulative enforcement of ethical rules upon psychotherapy, Neumann's "new ethics" tend to be denied by the return of "old ethics." One might even say that as a rule the administration of rules in such processing de-creates whatever the new ethics had managed to create. Rules, by coming to rule in this way, contravene analysis.

To be sure, general rules seem to ensure greater efficiency. For instance, exams are more efficiently and rationally administered if multiple-choice tests replace oral interviews. The individual response in all its particularity and nuance is sacrificed to the measurably swifter response that can be assessed across the board. It appears that psychotherapists have fallen under the influence of a similar drive toward generalization when dealing with ethical matters. Is that tendency acceptable, however, particularly among those who follow Jung's psychology, which puts the development and protection of individuality at its core?

From the collective standpoint—and because therapeutic professionals must deal with that standpoint collectively—it is unavoidable that handbooks of analytic ethics and the ethics codes of psychotherapeutic associations start off by speaking of general rules. They need to go back to—make a tactical retreat to—abstract generalizations. No human being, for instance, reaches psychic maturity at the same age as all others. Yet we conventionally decide, for the sake of administrative functioning, that from one's eighteenth birthday onward one will be fully responsible, else we would be in no position to punish and deter crime. *Per legem* we therefore revert to statistical definitions and statistical truth's limited value, which cannot strictly and wholly correspond to any single individual who comes within their view.

To draw lines in the outer world is an unavoidable and anti-psychological complication. Think of the borders between countries or even between private fields: borders between countries are never perfect or even fixed. They correspond not to natural law but to history, which is a perpetual displacer of boundaries. They are conventional simplifications, and yet even etymologically one face of justice turns toward them (among the many early usages of Greek *dikē*, or justice, one of them refers to divisions between plots of land). We must consciously suppress our longing for complete justice, then, and accept the convention.

Yet this acceptance is far from being something to take for granted. Boundaries are inherently anti-psychological, first of all because they deny the complexity of the psyche, and then because they reach a further degree of complication by enlisting in the service of the collective psyche. But in so doing they fulfill the unconscious need to simplify and govern this swarming complexity, for they encourage precisely the tension-relieving projections of guilt and responsibility. The denial of both complexity and personal responsibility can lead many kinds of people to speak of borders as something "sacred" and "untouchable." Yet the very expression "untouchable" in this instance must also be seen as a projection, for what is "untouchable" in fact is the rigid psychic balance of a fragile personality.

To draw lines in the inner world is an even more contradictory act. Lines and conceptual definitions tend to deny the intrinsic complexity of psychic reality. Yet even in order to describe the most typical case for which lines and definitions are unsuitable we have invented a suitable definition: borderline. Clearly, we stand in the presence of a major archetypal tension within justice itself, which makes a given *ruling* or line a live issue that invites dead or controlling identifications. The Greeks acknowledged this charged factor by placing little statues of the god Hermes at the intersections of plot boundaries: stylized phalluses of assertion, these herms also remained hermetic, double-facing, implicitly fluid signals to complexity. The collective human ego represses that complexity.

*I*n the typical, daily activity of psychotherapeutic ethics committees, we have traced without difficulty the tragic presence of the contradiction underlined by Jung: we aim at understanding, but we cannot help being coerced by knowledge and its rules—in our case, by the pretense of making an objective finding about responsibility. We could translate this into the specific field of ethics by saying: we aim at specific justice, yet we cannot help being carried away by general laws. We are helplessly psychological and anti-psychological at the same time. We are contradictory *tout court*. Does this imply that we cannot act ethically? Quite the contrary. We find ourselves instead in the ethical territory par excellence, the gray zone. In that zone we will never be able to claim that we have found the final truth, yet we shall always find ourselves standing in the landscape that is most apt for ethical elaboration.

As we pointed out, paradoxes and ambivalences are not occasional aberrations in analysis, its rare bad days. They are its structural ambiance and its everyday weather. Analysis, though it began only one century ago, does not presuppose Enlightenment, which is incorrectly assumed to be present, if not as a fact then as an inalienable tendency, in every manifestation of Western culture. Indeed, analysis is to a major extent not only a party to the pre-Enlightenment, but even to the pre-Aristotelian part of our mind. It is at home with that layer of the human psyche that does not pledge allegiance to the principle of noncontradiction. For the psyche in its totality (that is, including the unconscious), A can be A, but it can also be B, or non-A. I can be I, but I can be you at the same time. As we have said, the paradoxical dynamics of the unconscious are not an occasional virus we can get rid of, but our daily bread.

Ideally, the only way to come out of this predicament would be to replace all rules and regulatory codes with a case-by-case application of Kant's practical imperative for ethics.

Unfortunately, however, the realm of complexity stands ready to swallow us once again. Although Kant's imperative remains a pillar of modern ethics, every modern professional activity rests, to a certain extent, upon a suspension of it. As a rule, for the patient the professional is an instrument and not an end. From an ethical perspective, the fee the patient is paying to the professional is also the way in which the patient compensates for this instrumentalization.

Making a person into an instrument is probably, in itself, an archetypally unethical gesture, and certainly it engenders a debt. The payment tries to compensate for this (not by chance, both debt and guilt are expressed in German by the same word: *Schuld*). The more limited the role of the professional is, the better this correction works. Things inevitably get more complicated when this role is not only technical but also carries with it the whole personality of the professional (in humanistic versus technically specialized activities).

At the extreme of these humanistic roles we have the analyst. His or her tool is not just the drill, as in the case of the dentist, but the whole of the personality.[6] The patient might perceive the intervention with growing intensity, until it acquires a *totalizing quality*. The somehow instinctive but regressive consequence is a wish for a *total participation* of the analyst in the patient's life.

Should the patient uncontrollably express this wish during the analysis, then from a traditional psychotherapeutic perspective we call this attitude on the patient's part *acting-out*—"out" of the analytic container. Of course, behind the attitude might lie an unconscious adolescent impatience, or even a drive to sabotage the goals of analytic work. But from an archetypal ethical perspective, one might wonder if the patient's wish is not also an unconscious attempt to act according to the Kantian imperative. That is, the unconscious, archetypal drive of the patient might be refusing to consider the analyst only as an instrument of the healing process, insisting that the relationship with the analyst become an idealistic relationship of nonutilitarian love. In that view of things, the patient's psyche wants the analyst to become a person in the flesh, and so it tries to flee from the symbolic ground of analysis. In this sense, the acting-out perceived by traditional psychotherapy can also be seen as an unconscious move toward "acting in" the Kantian imperative.

Notice that from the standpoint of this unconscious drive in the patient's psyche, it is precisely the continuation of a boundary-conscious psychotherapy that, paradoxically, is felt as an abuse.

Complexities seldom come unattended. This move on the part of the patient's psyche might correspond to an opposite one on the part of the analyst. The "ethical-enough analyst" works well within therapeutic boundaries and therefore can allow a certain amount of countertransference respecting Kant's imperative. The patient, or more precisely the healing of the patient, is his or her final goal, precisely in the sense described by Kant. Usually, then, it is only if and when the practitioner enters a personal relationship with the patient that an instrumentalization of the relationship starts, hence incurring a breach of Kant's practical imperative.

$\mathcal{T}$he ethical imperative of Immanuel Kant is a humanistic one, deriving neither from abstract schemes nor statistical rules. Precisely for these reasons, it can offer a crucially important inspiration for our work as analysts or therapists. Unfortunately, we also need laws and definitions, and in the face of this dual obligation we need also to heed Jung's advice: "The conflict [between knowledge and understanding] cannot be solved by an either/or, but only by a kind of two-way thinking: doing the one thing, while not losing sight of the other."[7] The same goes for law and justice.

And so, when an Ethics Committee issues its rulings, we should bear in mind that they will evoke in us ambivalent feelings not because they are "wrong" but because the activity of such a body is structurally paradoxical.

All such analytic bodies must remain faithful, in this two-way manner, to the paradoxical laws of the psyche as they meet up with the Cartesian and functional laws of society. The application of both sets of laws to a given ethical case can engender among analysts the feeling of being wretchedly inconsistent, even dissociated. Yet, facing up to psychological difficulties in this dual manner is simply their task.

At the present moment a potential monster has begun to stalk our relatively just Western society. Its name is judicial fundamentalism. The face worn by this monster is pure, unfurrowed by torment, and apparently all-seeing. The frequent stalemates created by democratic rules, and also by a sentimental cult of human justice, have planted the unpleasant seed of this development.

The burdens faced by ethics committees in our profession can serve as a salutary reminder in this wider social context. By applying Neumann's more ample ethical teaching to the collective unconscious, such bodies have the complex task of agreeing to make a ruling while remembering—and, just possibly, reminding others to remember—that the ruling inevitably will be partly unsatisfying or disconcerting, and that it will also express both justice and the shadow at the same time.

CHAPTER 12

Sabine S. and Anna O.

One evening in 2003 I went to the movies to watch *Prendimi l'anima* (*Take My Soul*), a low-budget film by the young Italian director Roberto Faenza. According to the critics, the film portrayed the life of Sabine Spielrein in a slightly sentimental but basically convincing way.[1] By then I was also aware of the existence of the less commercial Swedish movie *Ich hiess Sabine Spielrein,* directed by Elisabeth Marton, and of the fact that *The Talking Cure,* by Christopher Hampton, had excited avid interest in London's theater circles. (That play also centered on Sabine Spielrein, although limiting itself to an imaginal reconstruction of her interaction with Jung.)

The widespread interest surrounding this specialized topic marks a new chapter in the historiography of psychoanalysis and, at the same time, in its ethics. Society at large, not only therapists and historians, is looking into the history of psychoanalysis and, incidentally but also momentously, into the history of analytical ethics.[2]

Sabine Spielrein was a Russian Jewess nineteen years old when she was admitted, in the summer of 1904, to the Burghölzli Clinic, where Jung worked under Eugen Bleuler. At that time, Jung had not yet met Freud, but was reading his work with passionate interest. According to psychoanalytic criteria, Spielrein's diagnosis was hysteria.

Sabine's symptoms as registered in the hospital's records at her admission reveal quite disturbed behavior. After ten months as an in-patient, however, she had shown astonishing improvement and was allowed to leave the clinic. Instead of returning to Rostov, her native city, Spielrein remained in Zurich, where she began studying medicine. Jung continued to meet with her as an outpatient.

During the following years the relationship between Spielrein and Jung became more and more intimate. Although its meaning has been variously interpreted, love certainly became part of it. Gradually, things got complicated by the difficulty Jung faced in keeping this intense experience alive while at the same time leaving his marriage and precociously successful career intact. The drama recorded in correspondence between the two eventually records the entrance of new players. Jung informed Freud about a very interesting "hysteria case" and also, later and reluctantly, about his personal involvement. While Spielrein's mother contacted Jung, both Sabine Spielrein and Jung's wife ended up writing to the Viennese master, who allowed himself to be drawn in.

In his correspondence with Jung, Freud seems more concerned about possible damage that might be done to the psychoanalytic movement than about personal injuries suffered by Spielrein, thereby colluding with Jung's defensive attitude. He advised his "crown prince" (as he called Jung) that there are certain costs in feeling to be paid for the advancement of their science, namely, developing a "thick skin" (*harte Haut*).[3] He also expressed the opinion that Jung should not blame himself too much.[4] In keeping with the fact that the risks of erotic transference and countertransference had not yet been highlighted by these pioneers, Jung evinces guilt feelings for potentially hurting Freud's legacy while seeming to play down his previous sentiment of "moral obligation" toward the patient, characterizing his own feeling as being "too stupid" (*zu dumm*), as if the issue were his own lack of understanding.[5]

Only after the irreconcilable political and ideological split with Jung did Freud seem to take Spielrein's side, while she insisted that her wish was that the two would get back on collegial terms. When this proved to be impossible, she carried on a collaboration with the Viennese circle. Later, Spielrein worked in Geneva and Lausanne and became the author of several important psychoanalytic essays. She also married and had two daughters. Once back in Russia, she met with growing difficulties in being a psychoanalyst under Stalin's regime. Because she was Jewish, she was finally killed by the Nazis during the successful phase of their invasion in 1941.

I have no wish here to enter into the historical controversy surrounding the Jung/Spielrein case. Also, the latest historiographic interpretations, according to which there may never have been any sexual activity in the relationship between Jung and Spielrein, are not to the point for our purposes either. In terms of modern ethical codes, independently of the existence of a sexual relationship, there was certainly a breach of boundaries. In terms of human feelings, a love relationship indeed occurred, which spilled over the rim of the therapeutic container and outside the concepts of transference and countertransference.

What is worth discussing here is the public perception of the case. The tales reenacted in film and on the stage have been received with an interest that has manifested itself in very different contexts. We can therefore infer that the story or history has activated something that all these different people—the principals, the interpreters, and the artistic redactors—have in common. In Jungian terms, something archetypal.

*W*hen I saw it, *Prendimi l'anima* had been running for several months, yet only by booking in advance could I obtain seats. The theater was packed with young people, perhaps bussed there from a nearby McDonald's. Although interested in the screening, I was also taken by them. When afterward I finally walked back through the streets, I kept asking myself: "Why are they so fascinated, what have they understood?" The film had received very little advertising; the packed attendance was clearly due to direct word-of-mouth contacts among the young people themselves.

One reason for their interest, I believe, lay in the fact that the film's director had set the stage in what we have called "the gray zone." In itself, this fact is hardly unusual. But it is quite unusual for the handling of a story with so many evident ethical implications. When it comes to moral issues, the entertainment industry always prefers clear-cut narratives that shepherd the public toward easy identifications of good and evil. This film, however, implicitly asked the audience to entertain a paradoxical question: "Would the sensational healing process of Spielrein have been the same without the sensational breach of boundaries by Jung?" As in most good narratives, the message was not a statement but a question: either a question without an answer, or one that allows only apparently contradictory answers.

As I made clear earlier, I am interested in the second possibility, in which both the question and the answer are forced back onto the proper ground of analysis: ambivalence, unsolvable complexity, paradox. From this perspective, the answer is yes and no at the same time. Jung acted courageously and despicably at the same time. This is the tragic reality of a real tale in real life—not of a Hollywood fable.

The reader has already undoubtedly understood that I am suggesting that the evolutionary "collective unconscious" was activated—in Italy, Sweden, and England where Spielrein's story was being retold—by the tragic quality of her tale. Particularly the young people of our day live in an anti-tragic world. It is no coincidence therefore that many young people were gathering in that cinema to meet up with that simultaneous experience of good and evil our culture represses.

Only that kind of experience can lead the new generation onto the proper ground, where its attention can be quickened and "ethical elaboration" can take place. If ethical awareness stems, as we have assumed, not from learning dogmas but from wrestling with morally contradictory issues—by working through the complexity of a gray zone—then the new generations risk being particularly ill prepared, because of their growing exposure to the simplifications of moral issues provided by the entertainment industry and so-called news organizations.

To be sure, the transformation of the history of Jung and Spielrein into a drama or film story is unavoidably a bit voyeuristic and commercial. But even so, the ethical complexity of the original history can be simplified to only a limited degree by such renderings. Gray also means vicariously experiencing black and white, but resisting either extreme and welcoming the middle where ethics live in equilibrium. Justice has been symbolized since the sixteenth century as a blindfolded goddess suspending black and white or good and evil in her scales.

And that fact—ethical complexity—has consequences for the original event as well. Historical reconstruction shows that with the "Case Spielrein," Jung achieved his most sensational therapeutic success, and that from it he absorbed the most fertile inspiration for his later theoretical developments. The treatment of S. Spielrein was the "case zero" of Jungian analysis, and became at the same time the paradigm for all ethics cases in analysis as well as for analytical and therapeutic healing.

Among the therapeutic professionals who have shown a growing interest in reconstructing the Jung/Spielrein case, Jungian analysts are understandably in the front rank. Their intense curiosity and deep desire to know more about the case are clearly due to a "genealogic-tree factor." Facts from one hundred years ago usually seem remote, but they instantly become actual and near-at-hand once we know that they concern our grandparents or direct ancestors.

While recognizing, as Jungian analysts, that the way we read the case has a direct bearing on all later professional ethics because of its quality as a "foundational myth" unearthed from the cellars of history, we still might hesitate to examine it from an ethical perspective. Reluctance to take a stand can be justified by claiming that ethical codes for analysts did not exist at the time of the Jung/Spielrein encounter, and that in principle no rule can be applied retroactively.

However, the Hippocratic oath had been in existence long since, and Jung was a medical doctor. I suppose that psychotherapists coming from a cultural tradition other than Jungian would be less reluctant to give an ethical evaluation of the case. Analytical psychologists face a special difficulty, I believe, that I would call "The Grand Inquisitor" archetypal factor.

The chapter on "The Grand Inquisitor" in *The Brothers Karamazov* is one of the most famous in Dostoyevsky's work. Christ has come back to earth incognito. Only the most efficient watchdog of the

Church—an old cardinal, head of the Holy Inquisition—recognizes him. He begs Christ to leave and let him and the official Church carry out their heavy duty in peace: the time is long past for his preachings about justice and love! Now comes the less romantic business of routine duty and the administration of institutions founded on his behalf. His presence is a nuisance, if not an outright threat. Order and—he implies—rules are more important now than the spirit. By leaving—the Grand Inquisitor also implies—Christ would do the best thing both for himself and future generations. If, on the contrary, he stays and starts preaching again, the Church might have to condemn him on the basis of the authority he entrusted to it, and of the rules they have woven around his lofty message.

Jungian analysts asked to evaluate this pivotal episode of Jung's life may well feel put in a highly contradictory position. If they accept the possibility of judging it, they permit themselves to give a negative assessment. But if they were to express a negative judgment, they confront their fear of reactivating the psychological prototype of the Grand Inquisitor. It matters not whether we know Dostoyevsky's chapter, for the situation he describes is archetypal. Any analyst in that situation enacts what the chapter describes, namely, the betrayal of one's own founding myth. Therefore every Jungian practitioner gets fascinated by it, and anyone else with a genuine instinct for psychological growth, such as the young cinema audience in Milan, can be likewise captivated.

With unsurpassed psychological penetration, Dostoyevsky conveys the image of a dark corner of the human soul. The reader automatically recognizes in this chapter something that could happen to him tomorrow, that is to say, a psychological situation that manifests an autonomous force and its own pattern of action. If the reader is a Jungian analyst, the bite of recognition goes in more deeply. Apart from feelings of guilt, the analyst could also be entrapped in a feeling of cultural contradiction. Enough historical research now points to the fact that those years and, more specifically, the encounter with Spielrein, were decisive in the development of Jung's ideas. Examining that event critically might make Jungian analysts feel as if they were denying their history, and sawing off the branch upon which they are sitting.

*L*et us now turn from Jungian to Freudian psychology. Here too, the "case zero" is represented by a relationship between a doctor and a young female patient, in which both transference and countertransference had gotten out of control.

The "case Anna O.," however, was not a therapeutic case treated by Freud, but by Josef Breuer, with whom Freud himself initially collaborated. It became the founding episode of all modern psychotherapy: for the first time, a case of so-called hysteria was declared as having been completely cured (as we will soon see, this verdict is disputable), and the cure was later explained by a theory that became the cornerstone of a whole new psychology.

Contrary to Breuer's declarations, we now know that Anna O. suffered from serious relapses. In 1925 Jung, making reference to a personal communication from Freud, stated in a seminar that there had been "no cure at all in the sense in which it was originally presented."[6] Ernest Jones, Henri Ellenberger and Mikkel Borch-Jacobsen have later added more information to the already complicated picture, but all of them have confirmed Jung's assessment.[7] As in the case of Sabine Spielrein, we will not go into the details of a specialized reconstruction. There are, however, several elements that directly concern the field of ethics.

Anna O.'s real name was Bertha Pappenheim, who is still remembered as a Jewish philanthropist. She apparently suffered a great deal after (or even because of) the interruption of Breuer's treatment, to the extent that she had to be hospitalized at the Bellevue Clinic in Kreuzlingen. However, she later recovered, and her life gradually became the success story of a woman engaged in promoting Jewish culture and relieving the conditions of poor Jewish women in Central and Eastern Europe. One possible way of looking at her life is to see her not only as the person who contributed to the foundations of Freud's theories but who also anticipated what Jung was later to call a process of individuation.

While historical research has progressed, the passage of time and two world wars may prevent us forever from fully knowing the story of Anna/Bertha and her therapy (which she herself named "The talking cure," thus indirectly setting in motion the methodological trend of the whole of psychoanalysis). Her involvement with Breuer was so intense that she experienced a hysterical pregnancy. His corresponding involvement with her is expressed by the fact that he apparently spent more than one thousand hours with her during the course of one and a half years. As in the Jung/Spielrein case, with such a degree of involvement the absence of sexual activity between therapist and patient does not alter the fact that reciprocal intimacy had gotten out of control, becoming threatening in many respects. A decisive factor in the interruption of the treatment was, most likely, an attempted suicide by Breuer's wife.

We are once again warned against the risk of constructing a separate professional ethics and letting it stop at the door of the psychotherapist's consulting room. If Breuer was trying in good faith to help the patient through unconditional dedication, was the well-being of his wife and family a justifiable price for that commitment?

And of course lying is unethical. But did Breuer lie when he wrote that the patient had been cured? Or should we take another, more general and symbolic perspective and declare that he expressed a sincere and clairvoyant overall conviction that she would be finally able to live a full and rich life?—which in the end proved true.

There is an important distinction established in ethics by Max Weber.[8] You follow a *Gesinnungsethik* (the ethics of conviction) when your criterion of action is good faith and firm belief. A *Verantwortungsethik* (the ethics of responsibility), on the contrary, implies that you will be accountable for the practical consequences of your action. In a certain sense, this second possibility is the harbinger of the "new ethics" described by Neumann at a later date, and might hint that the great sociologist was already taking into account the unconscious factors described by psychoanalysis, which in his day were rapidly spreading through German-speaking countries.

In order to attempt an overall evaluation of Anna O.'s therapy, we must revert to the basic ethical categories of Kant. Did Breuer consider the patient as, and nothing else than, a human being worth helping, or did he succumb to the temptation of making her into an instrument? Surely we must invoke that distinction.

Paradoxically, during the therapy he acted recklessly but also in good faith, as the explosive potentials of transference and counter-transference were not yet known. But after the official termination of the therapy, both he and, to a significant extent, Freud, influenced by the need to provide empirical grounds for their new theories, ended up instrumentalizing her case history. The paradoxical result is that, according to Ellenberger, the historic basis for the success of psycho-analysis was provided by an unsuccessful case.

If Breuer and Freud acted unethically, it was because they eventually placed the value of scientific research before that of a human being. This becomes possible only when one tries to turn the humanistic discipline of analysis into "natural science," as many analysts of the first generation were persuaded that it was. We may legitimately infer that an unconscious desire to control the new field, by subjecting it to "objective, scientific" laws, was animated by a power drive—typical of many great figures—that failed to take into account either the "new ethics" that would be appropriate or the possibility of being driven precisely by those unconscious factors whose study they were pioneering.

*W*ith Kant's ethical categories in mind, we can now return to Spielrein. For Jung, too, at the time he was treating her, was not aware of the explosive potentials of transference and countertransference. While we will never be able to reconstruct the event completely, and even less the inner dimension of it, we may find something convincing in the supposition that Jung, in good faith, tried hard and with all his strength, unsparingly taking every risk, in order to heal Spielrein—without having other aims. It is possible that the popular interest in current stagings of the Jung/Spielrein case is due largely to the fact that the writers and producers of these dramatic renderings have indirectly adopted this perspective.

Unlike Breuer, Jung did not later try to turn the case into a success story for publication and the diffusion of his ideas. But he did make frequent references to her case in his correspondence with Freud. We do not know how far the reciprocal seduction went in the therapy itself (it is more difficult to speak of abuse, as in those times the proper "use" of psychotherapy was not yet defined). But we can observe that Jung was partly acting in a seductive way with Freud, and bent his representation of the case to this end.

From this perspective, Jung (ab)used Spielrein as an instrument. With the arrogance of two men in a male-dominated era speaking about an absent woman, and of two men of power speaking about a powerless woman, the correspondence between Freud and Jung continued instrumentalizing and offending her.[9] In a condescending way, Freud took for granted Jung's illustration of the case, later referring to her as "the little one" in his letters to Jung.

Setting this episode within a historical perspective means also noticing that both men were in the grip of a positivistic illusion—of being on the verge of discovery in the inaugural phase of a new science that will establish unshakable laws. This was equally true of Jung, whose overall work went on to reveal a religious and romantic bent. Set in the scales with all of that, individual feelings, however respectable, seem frankly pathetic. This illusion falls into line with an intellectual bias visible in the Marxism, Freudianism, and Darwinism of the late nineteenth century, according to which individuals serve as the laboratory in which history will gradually supplant God and ensure progress as a final, secular faith. In Jung's own terms, there is a shadow side to this master-trend of ongoing Enlightenment, one that in retrospect we might call Endarkment.

Certainly, no great master of the therapeutic arts has been exempt from confronting this shadow factor. Each of them works under the constant temptation to conceive the treatment of their patients as a "laboratory experiment," which, if they succumb, lands them in Kant's unethical territory on both categorical counts.[10] In a similar way, the reconstruction of private lives can be a contribution to historical research, but likewise can go over the edge in order to satisfy the anti-Kantian predilections of our voyeurism.[11]

*H*aving raised the matter of machismo in addressing the male-dominated ethos of the Freud-Jung era, we can come to one last consideration. Because of male dominance in society, and because the first psychoanalytical associations were overwhelmingly composed of men, abuses in analysis have for long been (and probably still are) mostly sexual abuses of female patients committed by male therapists.

Having lacked power in society and the possibility of imposing their will on men, who typically tend to disappear after the seduction/ abuse, women have often regressed in despair to what we might call a "Dido archetype." The mythical queen of Carthage killed herself, swearing eternal hostility to Aeneas—who, after starting a love affair with her, suddenly remembers the mission the gods have entrusted to him, but quite unheroically prepares to leave without facing the desperate Dido.[12] It is tempting here to see an analogy with Breuer and Jung, who went back to the quasi-religious endeavor of science once the feeling situation threatened to get out of control (a corresponding masculine situation, which could be called the "Aeneas archetype"). Through millennia, society has instilled in women the notion that their heroism lies in the battle of love. Even a woman who is also a major public figure like Dido must center her life on the feeling issue. Hence, when the fight is lost, as honorable male heroes do on the battlefield, she too must be ready to sacrifice her life.

We have mentioned that Breuer's wife tried turning to this same last resort, and witnesses have asserted that this was the decisive factor that convinced Breuer to terminate the treatment of Anna O.—although we do not know to what extent his decision was due to love for his wife or fear of a scandal.

The Jungian school of analysis has several times been reproached for paying too little attention to the enforcement of boundaries to intimacy. I wonder to what extent history might have played a role here. History tells us that there was uncontrolled intimacy in the therapy of Spielrein, but that in the end, and in spite of the fact that their lives parted, she never showed real resentment toward Jung. In fact, she seldom missed an occasion to speak favorably of him, and she even tried to foster reconciliation between him and Freud.

The fact that the "case zero," the clinical archetype of Jungian analysis, was a success story in spite of personal suffering on both sides, probably influenced the whole thinking of Jung himself, and later of the Jungian school. Let us briefly reflect on this outcome and its implications. Unlike the apparent failure, to some extent, in the case of Anna O., which accords well with Freud's distance from women and his overall pessimism, the successful professional life of Spielrein and her faithfulness to Jung might indirectly rest at the origin of an often too-confident attitude toward the risks of excessive transference and countertransference in the Jungian tradition. The bifurcated traditions of Jung and Freud have to do not only with methods—the formalized understandings drawn up around these pivotal cases—but also with ways of acknowledging and assessing ethical complexity. The two stories taken together present the whole of something that neither story alone quite reveals. And that entire matter touches the whole being in each of us.

CHAPTER 13

A New Ethical Frontier

Ethical issues in psychotherapy have come to constitute almost an autonomous discipline.

As we have recalled in the previous chapter, while psychoanalysis was attempting to extend a new kind of understanding and control over the psyche it came across transference and countertransference: unexpected, autonomous, and powerful phenomena that could hold the therapist or analyst under their control. From an intrapsychic point of view, it was as if professionalism could suddenly be displaced by unanticipated and overwhelming emotions and, from an ethical viewpoint, by abuse. In a certain sense, abuse in such analytic situations occurs in different ways at once: from the perspective of society, the therapist could abuse the patient, whereas from a psychodynamic one, the therapist could be the victim of her or his unconscious. In the first part of the twentieth century, while analysis was being rewarded with therapeutic and cultural success, the frequent and well-known cases in which boundaries were not kept constituted a heavy shadow side.

A partly spontaneous international movement aimed at enforcing professional rules was thus set in motion. The movement had two cultural roots. On the one hand, feminism contributed to a higher sensitivity toward the problem, as the overwhelming majority of the abused have been women, thus reproducing in our specific field the more general inequalities of society. On the other, pressures came from Anglo-Saxon Protestant countries, particularly from the tradition of American Puritanism. The historically high level of tolerance in Catholic countries, for instance, likely would have let matters rest unchanged for a longer time.

As we have noted, by placing our ethical issues within the broader spectrum of general ethics we gain a broader means both for understanding them and for being consistent with ourselves and with the wider field of ethical concerns.

Acknowledgment of abuses in the psychotherapeutic field has been a decisive factor in its ethical debate. And the vitality of this debate reaches far beyond the specialized field of psychotherapy.

Historically, psychoanalysis and psychotherapy were both born in the cradle of medical studies. But, as we have already recalled, it gradually became necessary to recognize that they constitute a discipline epistemologically separate from medicine, their temporary foster parent. They belong not to the natural sciences but to the humanistic ones. The stamp of this truer genealogy also shows up in the history of their ethics.

Although the term "medical ethics" does not appear to be that old, when analysis was born the various medical disciplines had well-established ethical frameworks, running uninterrupted throughout Western history since Hippocrates (the fifth to fourth centuries B.C.).[1] But the infant field opened up a new ethical debate, in that it unleashed behaviors—and particularly emotions—that had not been anticipated. Of course, the phenomena of transference and countertransference exist also in the various medical professions, but there they tend to be expressed in much milder forms. With analysis, unconsciousness—on the part of both therapist and patient—becomes a primary factor. Ethical behavior cannot be confined simply to doing the right thing as opposed to the wrong thing. It implies also being conscious as opposed to being unconscious. A psychotherapist who acts correctly, by following the rules for responsible external relations, but who remains unconscious, does not measure up to professional standards even when, for the time being, there is no negative consequence in sight. In this greater perspective of ethical adequacy in analytic relationships, we must reconceptualize the idea of abuse.

Typically, what ends up as abuse on the part of the therapist begins as an action that is lacking not in well-intended goals but in awareness.

I now propose that we shift our attention from the idea of abuse to that of seduction. Seduction is the most typical root on which abuse thrives. Moreover, abuse is a judicial idea, while seduction is a psychological attitude: it thus belongs more properly to the field we are discussing.

Seduction is a complex issue. Not all seduction aims at abuse, for it works a much broader field, leading us into an increasingly gray zone. Plato, for instance, dismissed the whole of ancient Greek drama on the grounds that its goal was to flatter the public—that is, to seduce it and hence to manipulate it.[2]

As we know from his other writings, Plato customarily set very high—we are tempted to say unrealistic and somehow unpsychological—moral standards. Following a distinction often made by Jung, Plato's attitude could now be called "reductivism." Reduction takes place when one accounts for something of high value by means of explanatory terms derived from a much lower level: for instance, evaluating the paintings of Leonardo da Vinci as pathological expressions of his sexuality and not as works of art. Similarly—according to Plato—Homer, Aeschylus, Sophocles, and Euripides would have been driven by a "success syndrome" and not simply by a poetic drive. From our ethical perspective, Plato's harsh judgment almost constitutes a form of "cultural abuse." This charge, however, certainly does not need to be brought before any kind of judicial body. Time itself has been enough to settle the matter.

Nowadays we live in a world preoccupied with a constant flattering of the public (that it to say, the consumer), and we consider literature and art as the noblest expressions of this ingratiating appeal. We would feel honored, not offended, if Homer or Sophocles attempted to attract our attention with their work.

In comparison to the classical world, not only are we much more tolerant, we are also immensely self-indulgent. The goalposts and outfield fencing erected by Plato's Puritanism in his campaign against abusive seduction has been moved almost to another planet. In the name of personal liberty—and under invincible pressures from the commercial liberties that go with it—artistic production (quality aside) takes an almost infinite variety of forms (let us not forget that it was once disputed whether painting could hold its own with sculpture, as an art) and occupies an immense market niche. The fact that the artist offers a "creative"—as opposed to "industrial"—product, tends to excuse the excesses of the creation and guarantee a certain degree of esteem to the creator.

Let us now return to seduction. In accord with the path we have been following, we should try to understand it in the broadest possible sense, as an archetypal pattern in itself. Even independently of abuse and other clearly sanctionable corollary consequences, we may well wonder what seductiveness as such really is.

Its truly psychological quality is accented by the fact that it can be completely unconscious. It can form the manipulative, anti-Kantian shadow side of a transference and countertransference, both apparently filled with respect. The word itself reminds us that it is the first path toward abuse: the Latin verb *seducere* means to lead astray or away from the correct path. Actually, seduction can be particularly ruinous precisely when it is coupled with distinctly noble conscious intentions. This combination is typical of apparently spiritual, noble men, and has been described in narrative masterpieces, not by chance the work of likewise noble, creative men. Think of André Gide's *La symphonie pastorale,* of Henrik Ibsen's *Rosmersholm,* of Luis Buñuel's *Nazarin.* The shadow side of a minister's role is a psychological issue long before it ever manifests as a judicial one.

*D*uring the three and a half decades I have been working in both private practice and psychiatric institutions, my experience has spanned the cultures of three different countries. After having analyzed patients and supervised other analysts who come from many different backgrounds and countries of origin, I am now convinced that direct seduction by the therapist during psychotherapy is in decline, in most if not all countries.

But I am also convinced that humans remain what they are: that we are not becoming more ethical, for otherwise history would end up being populated by saints, and that really would correspond to the end of history! Rather than getting rid of problems, mostly we tend to displace them. Consider hunger, for one, which has practically disappeared from view in the West, but rather than being eliminated has been outsourced, as it were, to third-world countries.

Accordingly, I have thus started looking for possible avenues for the outsourcing of seduction into situations adjacent to analysis. My eye has been caught in particular by what happens before the patient enters into a relationship with the analyst.

When I started working, analysts—and particularly Jungian analysts—were scarce all over the world. They mostly led a secluded life, as if they were part of a spiritual elite. They were not eager to appear in public. Or, at least, they pretended not to be so, as some were already quite famous and had no need of exposure. A significant number of them were akin to the typical analysts of the first generations—that is, they were awkwardly introverted.

The "analytical market" was tiny or nonexistent. Most new analysts could count on contacts for referrals from the very beginning of their activity. At any rate, after a relatively short initial phase, referrals would come automatically from former patients. In this way, the analyst would simply have to sit in the office waiting for phone calls. Such a situation—let us call it an "introverted network"—enormously simplified what one could call "the analyst-patient relationship before analysis." It also suited the introverted temperament: we could simply remain what we were. This is by no means irrelevant for analysis, as very often there is an "anticipated transference," a transference that starts already in this pre-practice phase.

Not by chance, there is a whole literature on the initial dream of analysis. Very often, such a dream takes place directly after the patient has taken the decision to start analysis, or upon phoning in order to set up the first appointment, but *before* the first session. In the outer world, nothing has yet happened. But in the inner one—the ground on which most of the work will take place—things can be intensely in motion.

During the decades since I started working as an analyst, I have observed enormous changes in the process that precedes the outset of individual psychotherapy. The small psychotherapeutic market initially became a larger market, and then an immense one, mobilizing gigantic quantities of people and resources. In Western countries, psychotherapists became a veritable army. Inevitably, this army clashed with the phalanxes of the medically affiliated therapies, the pharmaceutical industry, and the lobbies behind them. The competition—both among analysts and between competing therapies—was escalating, and the task of finding patients was becoming more difficult. In this way, "the analyst-patient relationship before analysis" assumed the character of a growing, cumbersome, uninvited presence in the practitioner's life.

Let us now step to one side, into the daily reality of socioeconomic life. Popular idiom now parrots the formulae about our having entered an age of global free trade and the radically free market. But, as we have observed in speaking of Palace and Square in Part One, things are more complicated. It is true that many obstacles to free trade have been suppressed. But at the same time, as Jeremy Rifkin has vividly underscored, free access to the market is a thing of the past.[3]

The *market* was once a square in which one could buy and sell goods. Nonmaterial goods, such as professional services, were not usually offered openly in the square, but things worked nonetheless in a similar fashion. For instance, Harley Street became London's central market for physicians. Nowadays, material marketplaces are rapidly being replaced by virtual ones. In order to sell your wares, it is not enough simply to walk down to the square, and to sell your services it is not enough even to open an office in a certain section of town. To "be in the market" means to belong to a certain list, to have a Web site, to be known by the right people; being materially situated is no longer sufficient. You have to be previously known, to break through certain thresholds. You need, in Rifkin's terms, to have access to your potential clients. What you have to do, then, rather than be in the market, is to be in marketing.

If we now go back to analysis, we might observe that its marketing takes place within what we have called "the analyst-patient relationship before analysis." In such a space, professional or ethical rules of analysis would seem not yet to apply.

Or at least so we suppose, in order to avoid ethical complexity. This is not, by the way, such a new occurrence. Johannes Cremerius has unforgettably described how Freud, already famous and much flattered, allowed himself in turn to flatter the writer Hilda Doolittle, who had expressed the intention of moving to Vienna in order to be analyzed by him.[4] The most delicate of analytical phenomena—transference— might already be going at full speed during this phase. Transference— and of course also countertransference—can be blurred by heavy unconsciousness, and it is essentially because of these two mighty engines that ethical institutions of various kinds have been created.

As for marketing, it has created a relevant zone where unethical behavior can take place, but where protection from abuse has not yet been foreseen. Most typically, then, another *gray zone*.

Since the beginning of the psychotherapeutic professions, this zone has expanded enormously. Analysts offer courses, workshops, talks, and lectures. They publish popular articles, trade books, and answer readers' letters in magazines. They sell analytical activities not only to individuals, couples, and families, but also to companies. They interpret dreams online. They offer to assist the customers for special cultural events, trips, and vacations, at the slightest pretext.

The activity of many analysts has ceased to be linear, therefore, and has taken a circular form. It is hoped that the new, miscellaneous activities will bring clients into the analytical one. With time, these "collateral activities" might generate an income in their turn. The cycle completes itself when on the one hand the analyst's public activities foster an influx of patients while, on the other, the regular patients feed the analyst's collateral activities. At that point the marketing phase will have established a continuity—in both directions—with analytical activities proper. More and more therapists dedicate over 50 percent of their time to activities that are nonanalytical or nontherapeutic, but linked in this circular way to their professional practice; and these figures are on the rise. Because of this brand of circular continuity, there is no clear perception on anyone's part that the marketing takes place in a gray zone, and that from other perspectives one might see manipulation in its workings.

*T*he reader will already understand what I have in mind. Marketing is seduction pure and simple. The marketing of analysis is certainly less aggressive than that of material objects, but that fact hardly ensures that it will not be problematic.

Analysis used to practice underselling itself. A good rule of thumb given by an experienced analyst to the beginner was, "When new potential patients turn to you, be open, but not too enthusiastic. In the first interviews, check their motivations. You will never regret it." Nowadays, analysis tends to oversell itself: it announces loudly that all comers are welcome (although not necessarily everybody is suited for analysis).

Analysts try to entice people into analysis in an oversimplified manner. In the long run, as with every instrumental seduction, their trying too hard might have the paradoxical effect of alienating the public. In the shorter run, it ends up showing bad taste; and we have already made the case for aesthetics. Those engaged in such activities mostly do it in good faith, believing that they serve both their own interest and the general interest of their community. Seduction is not perceived as seduction, but as working for the common good. The common good, according to this perception, is the diffusion of an analytical or therapeutic idea. From the Kantian perspective, however, this would amount to the instrumentalization of the patient, justified by the attempt to spread an ideology. And by the same token, good faith has no influence on the objective consequences of the action for which, as Max Weber argued, one should be held ethically responsible and accountable. It is precisely unconsciousness that makes the problem of seduction our problem twice over: an ethical and a psychological issue at the same time.

When we hear that in buying a toothpaste we pay an 80 to 90 percent markup for its marketing and between 10 and 20 percent for the product, we are slightly horrified. At least, we are so to the extent that toothpaste can be associated with horror. Shouldn't we experience something similar, then, when we hear that an analyst dedicates anywhere from 50 to 70 percent of his energy to collateral marketing? Can the individual (meaning indivisible) mind be dissociated among such different tasks—serving economic and spiritual values—without losing some inner integrity?

Blindness on both sides extends the risk of abuse. The customer of this marketing phase projects an analytical trust (the "anticipated transference") onto the analyst, assuming that he or she will act with a healer's care. For instance, a participant in a lecture or seminar can tell an intimate dream to the presenting analyst, but the analyst does not feel bound by the strict ethical codes of the profession, because in this phase of activity the speaker is not acting analytically, but simply selling some immaterial product, like a specific knowledge. The ambiguity of the gray zone thus allows abuses that are not perceived as such.

Many other psychological abuses may be committed, against humanity as a quality of culture, although not against a human person. Every anthropologist, and with them Jung himself, has warned about the danger of extricating a myth or a rite from its native context and interpreting it within another one, for the specific purpose of some personal demonstration. Yet, this spiritual strip mining is occurring more and more frequently, specifically among persons who define themselves as Jungians. This misprision is largely a consequence of marketing, which allows for colorful but basically short spots, not for complex reconstructions of a cultural development. It is shocking to realize that this behavior recapitulates the practices of colonialism: using our privileged position, we Westerners "rape" (at least etymologically: the Latin *rapere*, to seize, describes abduction) some culturally rich but economically poor society, and (ab)use its mythology for our own interest. Something similar happens when we bring to one of our rich museums a mummy, and then express astonishment if one day an offended tribe reclaims it. Human mythology, spiritual culture, has its own life, and should be treated in itself as a human being: always as an end, not as an instrument.

For a long time, analysis has fought to keep seduction outside the therapeutic relationship, and to establish boundaries within it. The attempt thus far has been partly successful. Yet we should wonder whether this knotty and persistent problem has not gradually been outsourced into collateral fields, just over the horizon of our jurisdiction. A certain seduction seems to have been displaced and to have reappeared in the "anticipated transference," as I have argued here. And likewise the lack of boundaries, equally displaced, seems to reappear in the absence of fences separating analysis proper from what we have called "collateral activities," and even from among those activities themselves. It might be time to ask ourselves if such fence lines must necessarily remain external to our proper jurisdiction.

One innovation brought about by analytical ethics is the idea that transference does not automatically end with the termination of the sessions; therefore abuses can also occur after the end of analysis. But by now we also know that transference can start earlier than at the beginning of analysis. And, wherever there is transference there can be abuses of it, even before the official beginning.

Marketing—in a world that has depleted its vaunted "free time," and in which practically no space remains empty of objects—is almost regularly the attempt to force something onto a ground that is already occupied. Therefore, marketing supplants something already in place with something of a more questionable ethical nature, or of a lower intrinsic value, according to the economic law that says that a bad currency quickly drives out a good one, just as paper banknotes rapidly displace metal coinage.

Through powerful marketing, organized by powerful multinational companies, artificial milk proposes itself—with a whole series of psychological and sanitary drawbacks—as a substitute for the breast-feeding of infants, which will never have similar advertising campaigns at its disposal. Cooking with natural ingredients is hardly advertised and risks being replaced by highly commercialized and processed food. Nobody advertises writing, one of the cheapest and psychologically healthiest free-time activities. Nobody advertises a family that engages in good talk—a disappearing species worth several national parks.

But television advertises the watching of television. And in fact the entire entertainment industry tries to market products (commercial

TV is only the most visible) that expel from our lives conversation, reading, and writing. Food and culture get displaced by junk food and junk culture; the place of something decent gets usurped by something of both inferior ethical and aesthetic values (a further, unpleasant demonstration that ethics and aesthetics are archetypally linked).

Confronted with marketing, therefore, we should not rest content with asking whether its *form* is ethical, but rather if its substantial *goal* is. Not only should marketing prove that it is sincere when it praises something it wants to sell; it should also prove that the product it sells is not going to displace—to kill off—something of higher value.

Analysis has certainly been a great help to a Western world that, because of its economic and technological development, was already suffering from aggravated loneliness. But a too aggressive effort to sell it—more self-help books, more virtual marketplace therapy—might well further contribute to suppressing the delicate balance of those private communications that still manage to survive.

Such an outcome is certainly not what analysts want.

CHAPTER 14

Final Remarks

It is time to attempt to draw up some ethical principles for those who work as psychotherapists and psychoanalysts. Given the large differences between schools of thought and countries, we will have to limit ourselves to rather general maxims.

First of all, psychotherapeutic ethics should be, as much as possible, an organic part of ethics as a whole, not something specialized. The object of psychotherapy is the whole human being whom we conventionally call "the patient," not a specific part of his body or psyche. Also, the professional subject (I have added the adjective "professional" because both the patient and the therapist are "subjects" of the therapeutic process) whom we conventionally call "the therapist" acts therapeutically as a whole human being, not just from a professional capacity, or with just any specialized part of his personality. The personality of this professional is, like that of anyone else, an individuality: that is, something that cannot be divided.

Similarly, the ethical quality of both the therapist and the patient cannot be divided into parts, with one located inside and the other outside the consulting room. Both people are involved in the therapy as moral beings, not as characters who have to abide by certain rules as long as they act in a professional manner.

The sociopolitical roles of the partners in depth cannot be separated from their roles in the therapeutic situation, as matters to which they can remain indifferent.[1] An effective and ethical analyst, for instance, will not be capable of supporting violent political forms of society.

I remember the moving story told to me by a colleague from Latin America. During a phase in which a dictatorship ruled his country, he received an unexpected visit from a member of the secret police. This man had evidently been taking part in the kidnapping and torture of political opponents, and in similar illegal activities made legal by virtue of being ordered by the government. He did not experience conscious guilt, but suffered from sleep disturbances and anxiety. My colleague was torn between opposite drives. On the one hand, he felt an impulse of repulsion for the person and an equally instinctive fear of getting entangled in the knowledge of dirty secrets, thus exposing himself and his family to the regime's murderous way of silencing its adversaries. On the other hand, he felt a human and professional need to help.

Pondering the pros and cons, he decided to suggest to the "patient" that he should turn to the police's medical service. They would have both a duty and an interest in helping him, and could at least relieve him from the "heaviest" part of his own duty. Repressive institutions necessarily care a lot about collegiality. In such a case as his, they ought to be willing to meet his need for vacations and less oppressive duties, because otherwise they would be creating a difficult precedent. Inside the criminal regime itself, their activities could begin to appear ineffective, being seen to disseminate doubts and crises of conscience and not being automatically justified simply by virtue of following superior orders and collective goals.[2]

Most violent regimes need to pathologize these healthy forms of remorse and classify them as weaknesses.[3] For instance, it will classify soldiers not apt for frontline duty as suffering from mental disorders, not as individuals driven to express, as their last and just resort, their deep reaction to an illness and injustice that infects the whole of society.

My colleague explained to me that he, on the contrary, would have been unable to provide the policeman an exemption from "the frontline," which, given the circumstances, would probably have been the only realistic form of help. The policeman was a very simple man, without any visible capacity for introspection. He just wanted to get rid of his unpleasant symptoms and showed no readiness for self-criticism. Reflecting upon the case, however, I thought that my colleague also might have other reasons, of which he was probably not directly aware. Had he accepted the policeman for regular therapy, he would have doubted whether he was not somehow collaborating with the regime more than he would have wanted, due to the fact that a "symptom-relieving therapy" was likely to be the only instrument at his disposal.

"Psychotherapists" collaborating with unjust regimes have hardly ever existed, since one of the first concerns of tyrannical regimes is to limit not only outer but also mental freedom. Conversely, the constitution or ethics code of most psychotherapeutic professional organizations nowadays contains political principles of tolerance—clauses or preambles of nondiscrimination, on the basis of race, religion, ethnicity, sex, and sexual orientation—expressed in psychological form.

*F*or a long while I had an analysand who was the victim of a mafia organization. It would be out of place to reconstruct, here, his analytical process. A good deal of it pertained to normal life problems, with no connection to his dangerous situation. Here I wish simply to register the fact that I found myself in a condition in which my psychotherapeutic ethics and my ethics as a citizen were continuously entangled.

Besides anxieties connected with his childhood experiences, and his love problems or his difficulties at work, there was of course his constant real fear of being followed and eliminated. He knew certain secrets of the organization and felt that it was his duty to file a series of official allegations before various courts and magistrates. This of course exposed him to significant new risks. He would discuss that fact in analysis, mostly arguing that, after all, they wouldn't dare to touch him because he had deposited in a safe place even more information, potentially damaging for them. I believe that we both felt that this was a rather artificial simplification of the issue; but since he saw no alternatives, we tended to collude in pretending that it was true.

He was an ethically very consistent person, who would not give up the fight he considered as his life's task. But he was also relatively young and, in my opinion, he unconsciously overemphasized the need to be heroic. I tried to represent for him a more prudent approach, insisting that he had not only a moral duty to help the inquiring judges but also another duty to protect himself: that this other duty too was an ethical imperative, which had to be balanced against the other. With this attitude, of course, I was in my turn trying to balance my ethical obligations as a psychotherapist to individuals with those I have as a citizen.

One of his worst feelings was the fear of being left utterly alone. He had left his birthplace and was without relatives. He was also spending all his free time with lawyers, preparing his allegations to be brought to court. More and more, he found that the lawyers were deceiving him: they would spend long hours with him compiling and filing the charges and then, at the last moment, would withdraw behind a veil of technicalities. His logical conclusion was that they had been threatened. The only explanation seemed to him that they too were "on the other side" from the beginning, and had pretended to help him only to provide the criminals with detailed information about his charges against them.

I had also supplied him with relatively private possibilities of contact, such as my e-mail address and cell phone numbers, since he had warned me that he might have to disappear suddenly in case of immediate danger.

One day I received an unexpected e-mail in which he thanked me very warmly for the work we had done together, but said that he did not feel like coming any more because he thought—since indirectly I was becoming more and more knowledgeable about criminal affairs—that this was putting my family and me at risk.

I had to ponder things at length before answering and—unusual for an analyst—also consult with my family, which, without being aware, had become part of an extended transference/countertransference dynamic.

I did see his point. After all, it was the repetition of my own point from the other side. One has to find a balance between defending the rule of law against crime while at the same time defending individual life against unjustified risks. In the end I replied that I was very grateful for his concern, but that while I did not know to what extent the risks connected with potential "outer aggressors" were immediate, I did know that quite a few "inner aggressors" were ready to attack him, under the cloak of generous, sacrificial drives. I had committed myself to help him against them, and I saw no reasons sufficient to alter that commitment. In other words, I suspected that his renunciation of analysis could be also an unconscious, compulsive repetition of situations of loneliness and abandonment, which he had experienced since early childhood and which his present isolation, surrounded by menaces, was reactivating in terrifying form.

In hindsight, I do not know to what extent my analysis was objective. Possibly I overemphasized the psychological approach. Just as he had lent too much emphasis to the social one, so too I might have wanted to correct that imbalance. During our sessions he spoke mostly about outer dangers, and I of inner ones. But the distinction was sounding more and more artificial. I believe that I could not have helped him psychologically had I not believed that what he was facing was a horrible truth: in order to fight, every ordinary citizen, not just the heroes, must assume their part of the burden and its risk. Had I stepped out of the picture at his prompting, it would have been a small but bad precedent both for the ethics of my own profession and for the overall rule of law at one and the same indistinguishable time.

An ethical behavior that takes place in the consulting room but does not consistently extend itself outward into the therapist's sociopolitical life is a worrisome thing. But equally worrisome is a professional ethical attitude that lacks any real continuity with one's private life. We intuitively understand that a psychotherapist who at home beats his wife or abuses his children cannot be an effective therapist. Without our going as far as Breuer did, his example has already warned us that the problem of ethical consistency between private and professional life can arise very soon and quite unexpectedly. Breuer might have maintained the basic professional boundaries with Anna O.; but he still became too egoistic regarding his interest in her, at the expense of his family life. As we have seen, his wife's attempted suicide was a final bell ringing for him before it was too late. Something similar may be said of Jung. Even if it were proven that his involvement with Spielrein did not reach sexual intimacy, it had become too intense and appeared to be potentially damaging both his private life and his relation to Freud. In both cases, it has been disputed to what extent the problem belonged to the realm of ethics or to the domain of technique. But that distinction—like the one between professional, civil, and private ethics—is ethically dangerous. Only a person who has an ethical respect for the other person can learn the right technique that allows one to deal correctly with the other person, in this case a patient.

*T*he breaches "committed" by Breuer and Jung are the prototypical examples that show that there are no professional psychotherapeutic ethics distinct from nonprofessional ones. These pioneers have unintentionally taught us that ethical hot-button issues deriving from transference and countertransference pour seamlessly into the nonprofessional aspects of life.

We could call the principle that we are dealing with the necessity of a "horizontal widening" for psychotherapeutic ethics: horizontal in that it extends outward to all fellow humans, but also in that it should attempt to go on moving as far as humans themselves reach—which by definition is the ever-relocatable horizon—in order ideally to encompass everyone.

A second principle should complete the first, which would call for a "vertical expansion" of the horizon of psychotherapeutic ethics. This apparent oxymoron (etymologically, horizon and origin, Greek *horizon* and Latin *oriri,* both rest on the line where the [h]ori[gin] of the sun and our day is perceived) reminds us of what Neumann called a "new ethics": ethics that take into account not only the conscious rules of action we follow and the conscious goals we aim at, but also our unconscious omissions and all the complex unconscious motivations that can seize us at any step of an otherwise well-meant process—the dimension of depth, which tracks the sun's line into the dark. Ethics, therefore, that hold us accountable not only for intentional consequences but also for the unintentional and unconscious ones. This in its turn corresponds to what Weber has called the "ethics of responsibility."

How this second principle completes the first one becomes immediately apparent once we again reflect on the cases of Anna O. and Sabine Spielrein.

From the experiences of Breuer and Jung we are continually learning that psychotherapy cannot be a separate and distinct experimental field. The engaged therapist will often pour into it an enormous amount of his own energies and feelings. There will be an edge beyond which the balance starts to tip, leading to "horizontal" consequences: the other persons in the therapist's life will start to be affected. But very much the same considerations will meet us when we take up the vertical dimension. Over a certain edge on that axis, too, the inner psychic balance of the therapist will be overthrown: the ego will be pushed from the driver's seat. Impulses stemming from what in Freudian terms is called the Id, and in Jungian terms the shadow, will prevail in his personality; his life will be disturbed and, as a consequence, so will the lives of the people close to him.

The combination of horizontal and vertical principles helps us to perceive yet another general point. Independently of an (outer) respect for therapeutic boundaries, it is risky for any therapist, whether man or woman, to enter too exclusively into a professional task and thereby lose a decent inner balance between those specifically healing aims and the ordinary engagements with society and family. A "good-enough psychotherapist" should remain bound to those things as much as possible: being at the same time a good-enough citizen, aware of social commitments and engaged in them, and a good-enough parent and/or partner. Only up to a certain limit does the growth of that therapeutic engagement we call countertransference favor the therapy. Beyond a certain point, which is unknowable in advance and whose path cannot be reversed quickly or at will, it might rapidly damage both the patient and the therapist, in the latter case because it disturbs a human balance.

Freud expressed this principle by declaring that too much will to heal is wrong. And here we have made the point that there can hardly be an honest professional engagement if there is no engagement with society; but too much, too heroic a social engagement can also tip the balance, in that it fosters, as in psychotherapy, one-sided unconsciousness and hence a regression.

Both kinds of situation resemble that of someone trying to help someone else who risks drowning in a stormy sea or deep quicksand. The helper coming to the rescue must take some risk, and yet this risk should not be too heroic. If the rescuer is not holding steady or maintaining his attachment to some fixed point, he will be drowned or sucked down together with the person he is trying to save.

Linked to what we have been discussing throughout this book is a third principle, which ought to inspire all analytical ethics. It affirms the positive role of nearly every problematic and fascinating focus in psychic life, without scanting the corresponding energies of the negative.

To consider neurosis only in a negative sense means renouncing one of the richest possibilities of knowing what our psychic system needs, and consequently of helping it thereafter. Repressions and blockages are the unexpected, temporary walls that our daily journey can always meet up with. Neurosis holds its true meaning when we understand it as a failed attempt to reach a new psychic condition, which could lie just beyond those walls. Psychotherapy accomplishes its goal by helping not only to breach or sidestep the wall, but also to explore and conquer that new territory.

Equally, if ethics are not merely a last resort for dead-end situations in therapy, but a general inspiration for every psychotherapeutic phase and for growth in our psychic journey, then ethics cannot limit themselves to the negative, interdictive side: to repressions, prohibitions, and punishments. Ethics cannot be concerned only with the wall; it is in charge of the entire psychic landscape.

Historical experience in this sense does not deliver to us any definite set of rules, yet it does give us some inspiration. Countries with a traditionally high level of sexual tolerance—and which often do not censure pornography—as has long been the case in Northern Europe, have a relatively low level of sexual crime. As far as the consumption of intoxicating substances is concerned, generalized bans and generalized legalization of drugs have produced mixed results, but the prohibition of alcohol in the United States had to be revoked, and the limitations still imposed on its consumption are nowadays rare and considered mostly ineffective. If we consider the recent preoccupation with the negative educational consequences of indiscriminate media consumption by minors, we see that the hope invested in V-chip inserts as an answer to the problem has proven to be misplaced.[4]

Be it with minors or grown-ups, censorship alone—not coupled with an educational positive approach—simply halts the transgressive drive temporarily, without redirecting it. Usually it is only a matter of time until ways around or under the repressive wall will be found.

Let us now go back to countertransference, which is still the most frequent activator of unethical psychotherapeutic behavior.

Cremerius has convincingly reconstructed how deeply impressed Freud was by the countertransferential experiences of Breuer and Jung.[5] Having become aware of the danger of such experiences, he introduced the idea of *Abstinenz* (abstinence) as one of the fundamental tenets of psychoanalytic technique. The original Latin meaning of the expression *abstinere* has survived intact in the modern European languages, and belies a drastic negative implication: to keep (*tinere*) away (*ab-*). Freud's concern was not necessarily an ethical one: ethics as a category, in those days, was hardly used. More than technical and clinical, Freud's preoccupation was a political one.

In the letter to Jung dated December 31, 1911, Freud writes that Jung's article on "countertransference" is highly necessary, but should not be printed, remaining instead accessible only through private circulation among psychoanalysts. He was evidently moved by the desire to avoid any possibility that someone other than psychoanalysts themselves would become aware of the very concrete chance that a therapist might fall prey to an intense countertransference and start an affair with a patient.

Cremerius's summary of the evolution of the concept of abstinence shows how the rigid application of a rule ended up being almost unworkable, while it also underscores the fact that a too-loose application of a rule—which has been not only practiced but often implicitly accepted—provoked chaos.[6]

It is difficult to agree in depth with a principle that is exclusively repressive. Rather than be convinced, we will simply accept it—that is, be scared by it and submit ourselves to its authority. If its educational aspect goes missing, the corresponding "rule" finds very little purchase in the culture, failing to establish a deep collective consensus. It might remain essentially an individual inhibition—which of course can be spread to others, but only insofar as one also spreads fear. Once the fear of punishment eases, transgression resumes.

We might well wonder to what extent the frequently disappointing consequences of applying the abstinence principle in fact derive from its original negative conception.

Freudian analysis originally labeled transference as a neurosis. In its turn, Jungian psychology insists on the unconscious, positive aspect of neurosis. With this in mind, might we not find sound, creative phenomena that we can regard as archetypal models for what transference and its professional counterpart, countertransference—also called the transference of the analyst—unconsciously try to reconstruct?

We live in a secular and materialistic era, obsessed with possessions. Accordingly we assume that a love drive can only aim at the possession of the loved person. Yet before all else this attitude expresses a cultural limitation. In the groundbreaking poetic and literary renewal that took place in Italy and France between the thirteenth and fifteenth centuries, love was valued from a quite different perspective. It was a highly symbolic and radically creative experience: not materially, of course, but for the psyche. The core of that innovative culture was formed in Italy by Guinizelli, Dante, and Petrarca and became known as the *Dolce Stil Novo*—the Sweet New Style.[7] To it we owe a new philosophy of human creativity, which can be seen as nothing less than a refoundation of Western literature. For the *Stil Novo,* the aim of loving is not the possession of the loved person, but the elevation of the person who loves.

Dante saw Beatrice only from afar, who was very young and died shortly thereafter. What is essential for Dante is not this tragic destiny, but the psychic renewal inaugurated by the contemplation of her person. The brief presence of Beatrice in Dante's life transformed it forever and left in our hands one of the literary masterpieces of all time.

For the *Stil Novo*, the feeling of love in the sensitive person—through constant cultivation and the deepest dedication—can elevate humans to the highest orders of spiritual experience. Thus, that cultural movement simultaneously achieves two apparently conflicting goals: it clears the ground for a new spiritual and theological experience, embedded in literature and poetry and no longer depending on Church institutions and religious academicians; but at the same time it also elevates to the highest, divine level an important aspect of human feeling, originating within human experience and caused by a human presence. It thus lays down an essential basis for the humanistic movement, for the Renaissance and, further down the road, for the whole of modern secular culture.

At the same time, on a cultural and political level, it also drastically breaks with the stiffness and conservatism of the aristocratic world. The *Stil Novo* indeed creates a wholly new concept of nobility. Nobility no longer comes from birth; noble, in Guinizelli's words, is the *cor gentile*, the "gentle heart": the person with noble feelings typically described in the poetry of the *Stil Novo*, not the person born to aristocratic breeding, who might well be incapable of love.

Gentile meant in Latin "genetically noble." The word "genetic"—in English as in the other main modern European languages—still retains the meaning of "inherited through birth"—that is, born from a *gens*, a noble family (as in the English "gentry"). But from Guinizelli onward, in the Romance languages—and in English through borrowings from French—"gentle" will come to mean, on the contrary, a cultural and psychological quality, one that everybody in principle can possess, cultivate, and develop. From a political perspective, what at first seems simply a new poetic approach is actually the harbinger of the abolition of aristocratic privilege and the establishment of democratic qualities. At the same time, from a psychological perspective, the idea of gradually deploying the potentials of gentleness—through introspection and poetic exercise—can be seen as a first modern expression of what will then be called, in modern Jungian psychology, the process of individuation. Again from this point of view, the modern idea of individuation can be seen as the positive face on the coin of psychotherapeutic ethics: the activity to be accomplished, the natural balance offered to offset what should be avoided.

The new nobility unveiled by the *Stil Novo* is not a class of person that will engage only in the traditional art of warfare, as the blood nobility did. The new noble soul is capable not only of *destroying*; although brave in combat if necessary, this new nobility will on the contrary mostly *create*, in the renewed realms of literature and art. Its hallmarks will be the potential for democracy, a deep preoccupation with giving instead of killing, and immense admiration for feminine qualities—which were the inspiring source of all these new sentiments, and which obviously went hand in hand with the need to distance oneself from a masculine lack of delicacy and the implicit one-sidedness of the traditional warrior class. From this seed catalog one harvests much of what became the positive features of a later world.

*A*t this point we shall conclude by returning to Kant's ethical imperative.

Because it uses another person—the loved person—as an instrument for an "egoistic" goal (the elevation of one's soul), is the attitude implicit in the *Dolce Stil Novo* therefore anti-Kantian? Strictly speaking, the answer of course is *Yes.*

If so, is that attitude then abusive? The answer, equally strictly, is *No.* Not only was the object of the poet's creative imagination (Beatrice in Dante's case) not harmed by them, but she in her turn was elevated through glorification, although often unaware of it.

Kant's ethical imperative relies rather on a modern, post-Reformation and post-Enlightenment perspective. And so in a certain sense it anticipates our literal, reductive system of meanings, which eliminates symbols. It already negatively presupposes that humans will not be content with the psychological presence as such, and will want to take possession of what attracts them.

As I have tried to make clear earlier, the psychoanalytic perspective, on the contrary, retains a hold upon much of the pre-Enlightenment, pre-Cartesian, and even pre-Aristotelian world. The so-called Unconscious and, particularly, the Jungian realm of the archetypes, are precisely such prerational stuff. Archetypes convince us much more than logical argument can ever do, in that they correspond to our deepest, most ancient and symbol-related emotions.

The *Dolce Stil Novo* aptly bridged the insuperable power of archaic emotions with the modern need, and the right, to have individual emotional experience. It used the psychological presence of the other in order to trigger a new psychic condition, without nourishing expectations or claiming rights that would transform that presence into a possession. Often it learned to sustain this psychic responsiveness and tact even in the absence of any physical presence of the beloved.

As such, the *Stil Novo* represents the ideal archetypal pattern of a transference/countertransference dynamic, which fully respects both partner and boundaries, and which offers the paradigm of ethics that are not simply negative and limiting but more largely aim, with restraint as their springboard, at transcending the boundaries of our daily encounters, to receive and create meanings and symbols that survive the ephemeral human condition.

Notes

Chapter 1. Justice

1. *Nicomachean Ethics,* 1094 a and b.

2. Immanuel Kant, *Grundlegung zur Metaphysik der Sitten* (Foundation for the Metaphysics of Morals, 1785), BA52 (the categorical imperative) and BA66 (the practical imperative).

3. Jung, "A Psychological View of Conscience," Collected Works (hereafter CW), vol. 10.

4. Bauman, *Postmodern Ethics.*

5. Neumann, *Depth Psychology and a New Ethic.*

6. "Shadow: The inferior part of the personality; the sum of all personal and collective psychic elements which, because of their incompatibility with the chosen conscious attitude, are denied expression in life and therefore coalesce into a relatively autonomous 'splinter personality' with contrary tendencies in the unconscious." Jung, *Memories, Dreams, Reflections,* Glossary.

7. See Neumann, *Depth Psychology and a New Ethic,* chap. 1.

8. See Zoja, *Growth and Guilt,* chap. 5.

9. The Latin word *ius* (the etymon for "justice") refers to a universal right, while originally *lex* (the etymon for "law") was presumably simply a contract between two people or groups. Our modern use of these words—justice and law—seems to have preserved this original distinction.

Chapter 2. Beauty

1. See Buber, *Ich und Du* (*I and Thou*), part I.

2. In keeping with the intention not to separate the ethics of psychotherapy

from general ethics, I am anticipating here the typical situation one has to fight: abuse. Looking at things from a Jungian perspective, we cannot be content with a specialized study. We should set ourselves the task of understanding first of all the archetypal pattern of abuse. A similar approach runs through my study of addiction, where the archetypal pattern of addiction is studied extensively, before I address the specificity of drug addiction. See Zoja, *Drugs, Addiction, Initiation.*

3. See Toynbee, *An Historian's Approach to Religion,* chap. 3.

4. See Zoja, *Growth and Guilt,* chap. 6.

5. Various authors, in *Storia dell'arte italiana,* 2nd part, V (Turin: Einaudi, 1983).

Chapter 3. Palace and Square

1. See for instance in Niccolò Machiavelli's *Le historie fiorentine* (1532), Book II's description of the expulsion of Gualtieri of Brienne, Duke of Athens, and Book VIII's account of the conspiracy of the Pazzi.

2. "*Die gerade Linie ist gottlos.*"

3. See for instance Burckhardt's classic *The Civilization of the Renaissance in Italy,* parts 4 and 5.

4. See, among others, the *UNESCO Global Study on Media Violence;* the *Report on Children, Violence and the Media;* Browne and Giachritsis, "The Influence of Violent Media on Children and Adolescents," see n. 64, chap. 14; and the works of the German scientist Manfred Spitzer.

Chapter 4. Can Evil Be Avoided If Ugliness Is Compulsory?

1. Weber, *The Protestant Ethic and the Spirit of Capitalism.*

2. Williams and Zoja, eds., *Jungian Reflections on 9/11.*

3. Following Heraclitus, Jung calls this dynamic enantiodromia (reversal into the opposite). The implication is that both the inner (psychological) and the outer (sociological) processes we designate as enantiodromic do not represent the achievement of a new stage, but simply a continuation of the previous dynamics through the mere exchange of polarities.

Chapter 5. Has Beauty Been Shrinking throughout History?

1. Neumann, *Depth Psychology and a New Ethic*, Preface.

2. This phenomenon runs parallel to the privatization and isolation of literature, anticipated by Walter Benjamin in *Schriften*, Frankfurt: Suhrkamp, 1955). Narration and communication of experience are gradually substituted by information and entertainment. Traditional written narration is still reminiscent of its oral origins and preserves the potential of a two-way personal dialogue, whereas mass publishing and, even more, cinema and TV, become a one-way communication.

3. Aeschylus, *Agamemnon*, 11.788–89.

4. This idea is alive in most works of the modern American—but, at the same time, neoplatonic—author James Hillman, who poignantly pleads for respect for the eternal Anima Mundi in urban planning ("Practice of Beauty").

Chapter 6. Ethics Again

1. John Stuart Mill, *A System of Logic, Ratiocinative and Inductive* (1863).

Chapter 7. The Gray Zone

1. Levi, *If This Is a Man*.

2. Levi, *The Periodic Table*, "Vanadium"; Preface (1976) to the Italian translation of Jacob Presser's *Die Nacht der Girondijnen*; and *The Drowned and the Saved*, "The Gray Zone."

3. In my native city of Milan, historical research on the deportation of the Jewish community was shown in a recent exhibition (*Track 21, Milan-Auschwitz*). Before being shipped out on trains, Jewish families were jammed into the municipal jail. There they received—from both the guards and the jailed criminals—the solidarity the populace had not shown to them.

4. This would be another historical example of enantiodromia. See chapter 4, note 3.

5. Promotion of National Unity and Reconciliation Act, 34, July 26, 1995 (instituting the Truth and Reconciliation Commission): "there is a need for understanding but not for vengeance, a need for reparation but not for retaliation,

a need for *ubuntu* [a word in the Zulu and Xhosa languages that roughly means "humanity toward others"] but not for victimization."

Chapter 8. Narration

1. See Zoja, "Analysis and Tragedy."
2. See also Hillman, "Practice of Beauty."
3. Aristotle, *Poetics*, 13–14.

Chapter 9. Growing Unethical?

1. See Glover, *Humanity: A Moral History of the Twentieth Century.*
2. Rifkin, *Age of Access.*

Chapter 11. Processing

1. Jung, *Practical Use of Dream Analysis*, CW, vol. 16.
2. See note 6 in chapter 1.
3. Jung, *Undiscovered Self*, CW, vol. 10, paragraphs 493, 494, and 495.
4. Glover, *Humanity: A Moral History of the Twentieth Century.*
5. On "human resources," see ibid., part 1; and ibid.: parts 5 and 6 discuss, respectively, the weakening "drifts" under both communist and fascist regimes.
6. See, in this sense, the classical explanation contained in Szasz, *Ethics of Psychoanalysis*, part 1, chap. 2.
7. Jung, *Undiscovered Self*, CW, vol. 10, paragraph 496.

Chapter 12. Sabine S. and Anna O.

1. As mentioned in the Foreword, this is the same person who is often cited in English language texts as Sabina.
2. See Carotenuto, *A Secret Symmetry*, and Kerr, *A Most Dangerous Method.*
3. Freud to Jung, June 7, 1909. In *The Freud/Jung Letters.*
4. Freud to Jung, June 18, 1909, in ibid.
5. Freud to Jung, June 12, 1909, in ibid.
6. Jung, *Analytical Psychology*, Lecture 3, 16.

7. Jones, *Life and Work of Sigmund Freud,* vol. 1; Ellenberger, *Discovery of the Unconscious;* Borch-Jacobsen, *Souvenirs d'Anna O.*

8. *Politik als Beruf* (1919). Originally delivered as a lecture in Munich at the Freistudentisches Bund.

9. Jung to Freud, June 4, 1909, in *The Freud/Jung Letters;* Freud to Jung, June 7, 1909, in ibid; Jung to Freud, June 12, 1909, in ibid; etc.

10. See Freud's letter to Jung, June 18, 1909, in ibid.

11. For instance, the most complete source of information on Sabine Spielrein is Covington and Wharton, eds., *Sabina Spielrein: Forgotten Pioneer of Psychoanalysis.* The book is full of useful information, which I have partly referred to, but also contains many private details that do not add real substance. One is left wondering if, through their assiduous work, the editors have not identified too much with both Freud and Jung, reenacting their lack of respect for Spielrein by falling into what I have elsewhere called "writer's transference."

12. Virgil, *Aeneid,* books I–IV.

Chapter 13. A New Ethical Frontier

1. The term "medical ethics" first appeared in England, with Thomas Percival's *Medical Ethics: Or, a Code of Institutes and Precepts, Adapted to the Professional Conduct of Physicians and Surgeons* (1803). See Jonsen, *A Short History of Medical Ethics,* chap. 5.

2. Plato, *Gorgias,* 501–502.

3. See Rifkin, *Age of Access.*

4. Cremerius, *Die psychoanalytische Abstinenzregel: Von regelhaften zum operationalen Gebrauch.* See also Doolittle, *Tribute to Freud.*

Chapter 14. Final Remarks

1. On this topic see the classical text of Samuels, *Political Psyche.* Another important study dedicated to the correspondence between political situations and psychotherapy is Benasayag and Schmit, *Les passions tristes: Souffrance psychique et crise sociale.* Speaking of the impressive growth of juvenile psychic suffering, these authors highlight the need for psychotherapists to understand and also try to influence the social background.

2. I have described a similar case in an early publication, as a syndrome of "unconscious conscientious objection." See *Potere e inconscio* (various authors).

3. See Glover, *Humanity: A Moral History of the Twentieth Century*, chaps. 5 and 6.

4. See Browne and Giachritsis, "The Influence of Violent Media on Children and Adolescents," 702–710.

5. See Cremerius, *Die psychoanalytische Abstinenzregel: Von regelhaften zum operationalen Gebrauch*.

6. In her memoirs, Margaret Mahler reveals without apparent hesitation that A. Aichorn had been, at the same time, her training analyst at the Vienna Psychoanalytic Institute and her lover. See *The Memoirs of Margaret S. Mahler*, chap. 4.

7. Term first used by Dante, pronounced in *The Comedy* by the poet Bonagiunta Orbicciani, *Purgatory*, 24, 19–63.

Bibliography

Note: References to works by Aeschylus, Aristotle, Dante, Kant, Machiavelli, Mill, Plato, and Virgil are not specific to any edition, and are sometimes tied to uniform scholarly paragraph and section numbers.

Bauman, Zygmunt. *Postmodern Ethics.* Cambridge, MA and Oxford, UK: Blackwell, 1993.

Benasayag, Miguel, and Gérard Schmit. *Les passions tristes: Souffrance psychique et crise sociale.* Paris: La Découverte, 2003.

Borch-Jacobsen, Mikkel. *Souvenirs d'Anna O.: Une mystification centenaire.* Paris: Aubier, 1995.

Browne, Kevin D., and Katherine Hamilton Giachritsis. "The Influence of Violent Media on Children and Adolescents: A Public-Health Approach." *The Lancet* 365 (2005): 702–10.

Buber, Martin. *I and Thou* [*Ich und Du.* Leipzig: Insel-Verlag, 1923]. Translated by Walter Kaufmann. New York: Scribner's, 1970.

Burckhardt, Jacob. *The Civilization of the Renaissance in Italy* [*Die Kultur der Renaissance in Italien,* 1860]. Translated by S. G. C. Middlemore. New York: Modern Library, 2002.

Carotenuto, Aldo. *A Secret Symmetry: Sabina Spielrein between Jung and Freud.* New York: Pantheon, 1982.

Covington, Coline, and Barbara Wharton, eds. *Sabina Spielrein: Forgotten Pioneer of Psychoanalysis.* New York: Brunner-Routledge and Hove, 2003.

Cremerius, Johannes. *Die psychoanalytische Abstinenzregel: Von regelhaften zum operationalen Gebrauch.* Hamburg: Lecture at the Michael Balint Institut, February 25, 1983.

Doolittle, Hilda. *Tribute to Freud* [1956]. New York: New Directions, 1984.

Ellenberger, Henri. *The Discovery of the Unconscious: The History and Evolution of Dynamic Psychiatry.* New York: Basic Books, 1970.

The Freud/Jung Letters. Edited by W. McGuire. London: Princeton/Bollingen and Hogarth/Routledge, 1974.

Glover, Jonathan. *Humanity: A Moral History of the Twentieth Century.* New Haven, CT: Yale University Press, 1999.

Hillman, James. "The Practice of Beauty." In *Uncontrollable Beauty: Toward a New Aesthetics.* Edited by B. Beckley and D. Shapiro. New York: Allworth, 1998.

Jones, Ernest. *The Life and Work of Sigmund Freud* [1953]. New York: Basic Books, 1981.

Jonsen, Albert R. *A Short History of Medical Ethics.* New York: Oxford University Press, 2000.

Jung, Carl Gustav. *Analytical Psychology: Notes of the Seminar Given in 1925.* Edited by William McGuire. Princeton, NJ: Princeton University Press/Bollingen, 1989.

———. *Memories, Dreams, Reflections.* Recorded and edited by A. Jaffé. New York: Pantheon, 1961.

———. *The Practical Use of Dream Analysis* [1934]. *Collected Works* (hereafter CW), vol. 16. Princeton, NJ: Princeton University Press and Bollingen, 1966.

———. "A Psychological View of Conscience" [1958]. CW, vol. 10. Princeton, NJ: Princeton University Press and Bollingen, 1964.

———. *The Undiscovered Self* [1957], CW, vol. 10. Princeton, NJ: Princeton University Press and Bollingen, 1964.

Kerr, John. *A Most Dangerous Method: The Story of Jung, Freud, and Sabina Spielrein.* New York: Knopf, 1993.

Levi, Primo. *The Drowned and the Saved* (1986). New York: Vintage, 1989.

———. *If This Is a Man* [*Se questo e un uomo,* 1947]. New York: Abacus, 1987.

———. *The Periodic Table* [*Il sistema periodico,* 1975]. New York: Schocken, 1995.

Mahler, Margaret. *The Memoirs of Margaret S. Mahler.* Compiled and edited by Paul E. Stepansky. New York: Free Press, 1988.

Neumann, Erich. *Depth Psychology and a New Ethic* [*Tiefenpsychologie und neue Ethik,* 1948]. Boston: Shambhala, 1990.

Rifkin, Jeremy. *The Age of Access.* New York: Jeremy P. Tarcher/Putnam, 2000.

Samuels, Andrew. *The Political Psyche.* London and New York: Routledge, 1993.

Storia dell'arte italiana, 2nd part. Turin: V. Einaudi, 1983.

Szasz, Thomas S. *The Ethics of Psychoanalysis: Theory and Method of Autonomous Psychotherapy.* New York: Basic Books, 1965.

Toynbee, Arnold. *An Historian's Approach to Religion.* London and New York: Oxford University Press, 1956.

UNESCO Global Study on Media Violence; the Report on Children, Violence and the Media. U.S. Senate Committee on the Judiciary, September 1999.

Weber, Max. "The Profession and Vocation of Politics" (lecture of 1919). In *Weber: Political Writings.* Edited by Peter Lassman and Ronald Speirs. Cambridge and New York: Cambridge University Press, 1994.

———. *The Protestant Ethic and the Spirit of Capitalism,* 2nd ed. [*Die protestantische Ethik und der Geist des Kapitalismus,* 1904]. London: Routledge, 2001.

Williams, Donald, and Luigi Zoja, eds. *Jungian Reflections on 9/11: A Global Nightmare.* Einsiedeln, Switzerland: Daimon, 2002.

Zoja, Luigi. "Analysis and Tragedy" (1999). In *Cultivating the Soul.* London: Free Association, 2005.

———. *Drugs, Addiction, Initiation: The Secret Search for Ritual,* 2nd ed. Einsiedeln, Switzerland: Daimon, 2000.

———. *Growth and Guilt: Psychology and the Limits of Development.* London and New York: Routledge, 1995.

———. "Un caso de problematica etica inconscia." In *Potere e inconscio* (various authors). Milan: Formichiere, 1979.

Index

integration, psychological, and ethics, 5

intentions vs. accountability for actions, 78, 90–91, 100–101

introverted network of analysts, 87

Italy, post-WWII cultural transformation, 24, 29–30

Japan, post-WWII cultural transformation, 24

Jewish monotheism, 9

Judeo-Christian vs. Jungian psychological ethics, 4–5

judicial fundamentalism, 69

Jung, Carl Gustav: on Anna O. case, 77; and centrality of ethics, 4; *enantiodromia,* 110*n*3; on knowledge and understanding, 68; on social value of analysis, 55–56; and Spielrein, 71–72, 79–80, 81–82, 100; universal theory vs. individual situations, 56

justice: in ancient Western cultures, 7–8, 15; and gray zone, 75; psychological primacy of, 6–7; vs. rules, 54–55, 65, 66. *See also* ethics

kalokagathia (beauty and goodness), 9, 11, 15, 16, 17

Kant, Immanuel, 3–4, 57, 67

knowledge vs. understanding, 56–57, 64, 66, 68

law vs. ethics: ancient precedent for, 7–8; lack of balance in rule of law, 17; and natural vs. humanistic disciplines, 53–57; positive law, 8; practical effects of, 102–103; and religion, 76; rule of law vs. law of psyche, 69. *See also* rule-based ethics

Levi, Primo, 35, 53–55

lies, analysis as revealer of, 33. *See also* shadow

love as possession vs. elevation, 104–105

Machiavelli, Niccoló, 13

market, loss of free access to, 88

marketing, ethical complexities of, 85–93

Marx, Karl, 25

masculine, the, 14, 80–81

media, lack of aesthetic in, 17–18. *See also* entertainment

medical ethics, 84

modernism: anti-humanistic bias of, 64; arrogance in political power of, 13; and Axis nations' loss of culture, 24–25; and Enlightenment, 4, 66, 80; and loss of *piazza,* 13–15, 17–19; and privatization of aesthetics, 30–31

moral values. *See* ethics

Müller, Dr., 54–55

mythology, psychological abuse of, 91

narration, public-to-private transition of, 39–41, 111*n*2

national cultures, post-WWII denial by Axis nations, 23–25

natural vs. humanistic sciences, 53–57, 79, 84

Neumann, Erich: on cultural revolution of Jungian psychology, 4–5; ethics and shadow, 40; and loss of communal ethical base, 44–45; new ethics approach, 8, 58, 61, 63, 64, 78, 100; potential for redemption of underdog, 29; on psychological basis for justice, 8

neurosis, 102, 104

new ethics, Neumann's, 8, 58, 61, 63, 64, 78, 100

nobility, transformation by love, 105–106
nonpersonal extensions of therapy, 89–90, 92

opposites, tension of: *enantiodromia*, 25, 36, 110*n*3; and positive/negative polarities of therapy, 102; transcendence of, 68–69, 74

palazzo (palace): aesthetic contribution to community, 11; control of market by, 31, 44; and modern art consumption, 18–19; vs. *piazza*, 14–15; and political power, 13; TV as, 18
Pappenheim, Bertha (Anna O.), 78–79, 82, 99–100
paradox in ethical violations of therapeutic relationship, 57–69, 74, 78–79
patient as whole human being, 95–99. *See also* transference/countertransference dynamic
patriarchy and ethical violations of women patients, 80–81
Periodic Table (Levi), 54–55
piazza (public square), 11–12, 13–19, 30, 44, 45
Plato, 85
political life: arrogance of modern political power, 13; democratization of nobility, 105–106; media's control over, 18; need for beauty in, 21; and public art during Renaissance, 12
positive law, 8
positivistic illusion, Freud and Jung's, 80
possession, love as, 104–105
postmodern society, balance of ethics and aesthetics in, 26

practical imperative, 3–4, 57, 58, 67, 106
Prendimi l'anima (Take My Soul) (Faenza), 71, 73–74
privatization: of aesthetics, 29–30; of narration, 39–41, 111*n*2
processing of ethical breaches in analysis, 53–69
projection: of shadow, 56, 61; and simplification of psyche, 65–66
psyche: ambivalence of, 40–41, 57, 66–67; loss of shadow, 44; rule of law vs. law of psyche, 69; simplification of, 65–66, 90. *See also* unconscious
psychology. *See* analysis
psychotherapy, xvii–xviii, 34, 39, 45, 97. *See also* analysis
public life: lack of communal aesthetic in, 18–19, 30–31; loss of narration in, 39–41, 111*n*2; and *piazza*, 11–12, 13–19, 30, 44, 45
Puritanism, 22–23, 84

rationality: and Enlightenment influence on psychology, 4, 66, 80; natural vs. humanistic sciences, 53–57, 79, 84. *See also* modernism
reductivism, 85
Reformation and loss of aesthetics, 22–23
relationship, therapeutic. *See* therapeutic relationship
relativism and justice, 8
religion: and aesthetics, 10–12, 26; American civil, 24; as ethical guide, 4–5; Greco-Roman polytheism, 7–8, 9, 22; historical shifts in relationship to ethics, 5–6; Jewish monotheism, 9; and law vs. ethics, 76; and manipulation of patients, 58; and psychological primacy of justice, 7. *See also* Christianity

Other books in the
Carolyn and Ernest Fay
Series in Analytical Psychology

ISBN-13: 978-1-58544-578-3
ISBN-10: 1-58544-578-9

52395